PRAISE

"Anyone who wants to succeed in business and life will do well to read this book. Ed Mendlowitz packs the pages with suggestions and insights that can be found nowhere else. This is a valuable book."

> **Robert L. Dilenschneider,**
> **chairman and founder,**
> **The Dilenschneider Group, Inc.**

"What is included certainly is a compilation of what Ed has discussed with me and constitutes a primer on dealing with life and business and the necessary balance between both. The parts referring to communication are particularly relevant. I enjoyed the book immensely."

> **Edward Burak,**
> **IFM, president,**
> **Hudson Awning & Sign Co., Inc.**

"Ed has an impeccable knack for imparting common-sense nuggets that lead to a better sense of self and beyond that—to dollars-and-cents!!"

> **Sharon King Hoge,**
> **consumer consultant**

"In keeping with Ed's theme *short and to the point advice*, let me just say **READ THIS BOOK!** Ed *talks the talk AND walks the walk!* His talking and walking made it easy for me to *Listen and Run! Power Bites* not only will help you be more successful, it will help you be a better person! Read it and then give it to your kids to read as well."

> **Philip Goldschmiedt,**
> **president & CEO,**
> **Poly-Version, Inc.**

"*Power Bites* is a creative way of delivering sound advice. The book is full of humor so the reader can learn and enjoy at the same time. It is a quick read and I would recommend it for all levels of management."

> **Maureen DeCicco,**
> **partner,**
> **WithumSmith+Brown**

"The anecdotal reminders are a definite *must read* for any business executive. It's a positive "eye-opener" of advice relevant to any enterprise. Anyone, whether new to a position or with many years experience, will gain insight and confidence from this book. As I read, I felt Ed was personally looking over my shoulder and guiding me to the correct decisions for success in business, as he has for many years."

H. G. Clarke,
P.E., chairman and founder,
Clarke Engineering Company, Inc.

"I really enjoyed reading *Power Bites*. Ed Mendlowitz has been our accountant for almost ten years. His advice is priceless."

Gity Birnbaum,
CFO, Birns Telecommunications, Inc.

"*Power Bites* is a great read. Ed provides terrific advice about how to lead a more focused life, manage a more efficient business and better focus on the important things in life. I highly recommend this book."

Steven Rubenstein,
president, Arrow Partners, Inc.

"I have always enjoyed and admired the many things Ed does and has accomplished. His insights, ideas, and advice are always clear and 'right on'—yet, at the same time, paint a broad brushstroke that always applies, and connects to all, and *Power Bites* is an extension of Ed's counsel and guidance."

Christine Jaguin Iaderosa,
design consultant and artist

"*Power Bites* gives Ed Mendlowitz's formula for success. He has been my accountant, confidant, and friend for over twenty-five years and lives his life as an honest, accomplished accountant and great leader. This is a must read, how-to book for anyone who wishes to be a successful business person, professional, manager, and leader.

Dr. Robert M. Lipp, DPM

"Ed's new book gets right down to the critical issues that every manager needs to know in an easy to absorb and retain format."

Art Hein, managing director, Jarchem Industries, Inc.

"Ed Mendlowitz, the best accountant I have ever known, now gives us his best book, *Power Bites*. Combining both wit and sagacity, *Power Bites* is insightful, pithy—and a delightful read."

Jeannette Scollard, writer/author

Power Bites is a great compilation of things we'd all like to believe we do each day but really, if we're being honest, we need a reminder like this to help us fine-tune our everyday dealings in both our personal and professional lives. Being the founder of auntieup.com, I especially liked chapter 46—Call Your Aunt.

**Gina I. Samuels,
marketer extraordinaire,
founder www.auntieup.com**

"I approached this book with a bit of skepticism as to how it would be relevant to my profession; however, I completed it with a new outlook on both my personal and professional life. With over four decades as a CPA, Mr. Mendlowitz was able to not just create a "business plan" but a "life plan.""

Peter K. Zakow, MD

POWER BITES

*Short and to the Point Management, Leadership,
and Lifestyle Advice I Give My Clients!*

EDWARD MENDLOWITZ, CPA
Partner, WithumSmith+Brown

iUniverse, Inc.
New York   Bloomington

Power Bites

iUniverse books may be ordered through booksellers or by contacting:

iUniverse
1663 Liberty Drive
Bloomington, IN 47403
www.iuniverse.com
1-800-Authors (1-800-288-4677)

ISBN: 978-1-4502-2444-4 (sc)
ISBN: 978-1-4502-2443-7 (dj)
ISBN: 978-1-4502-2445-1 (ebook)

Library of Congress Control Number: 2010905159

Printed in the United States of America

iUniverse rev. date: 04/19/2010

To Ronnie,
who advises me!

CONTENTS

PART III
DELEGATING

PART IV
EFFICIENCY

PART V
BUSINESS DEVELOPMENT

PART VI
NEGOTIATING

PART VII
YOU

PREFACE
Reflections on reaching the traditional (for everyone else but not for me) retirement age

Edward Mendlowitz, certified public accountant. That has been my identity for forty-four years—a proud member of a proud profession.

Growing up, I always wanted to be a CPA, like my father. When my friends played house, I played accountant. It has been a lifelong dream, and I am grateful to say that I lived my dreams.

Public accounting is an amazing, challenging, and cool profession. I can honestly say that I have had very few bad days and eagerly looked forward to the work—the continuous learning, the clients who have been among the smartest of people you could work with, and the colleagues you interact with daily.

The excitement for me has not been who my clients have been, but what I could do for them. I think the thing that made me successful has been an ego that would not permit me to fail to do my best in everything that I worked on, combined with a basic insecurity that every time a client called it would be to discharge me. I rarely left a client meeting without thinking of what I would do next for them, and I never entered a meeting unprepared.

Exciting moments also included seeing young associates getting that spark showing that "they got it!"; creating systems that simplified the work with greater output and information; telling a client something they did not know about their business, enabling them to grow and earn greater profits; helping a family properly plan and become more secure; and assisting fellow accountants in improving their practices.

In my career I have been fortunate and blessed to have worked for and with the best in our profession, to have had partners that accommodated my simultaneous and conflicting creativity and process-oriented desires, to have had parents that encouraged me to not be afraid to try, and to have had a wife that became my lifelong friend and partner, soul mate, and stabilizer, who made everything I did worthwhile.

ACKNOWLEDGMENTS

Thousands of the people I've interacted with have put tens of thousands of ideas into my head that I use regularly. This book is a true collaboration with every one of them. Following are some whom I specifically recall part of their great contributions.

Ronnie Mendlowitz—nothing I do can be accomplished without her encouragement, love, and support.

Andrew D. Mendlowitz, Richard C. Mendlowitz, Amy L. Mendlowitz, Jake Ansel, David Bahr, Walter Bialo, Randy Bruce Blaustein, Ronald Bleich, Frank R. Boutillette, Reverend Dr. Ken Cadette, Ruben Cardona, Joseph Carroll, Clarice, Robert L. Dilenschneider, Martin Edelston, Rabbi Richard Fagan, Howard Fein, Maureen DeCicco, Bill Hagaman, Alan Heller, Stanley Hochhauser, Bernard D. Kleinman, Sherman Kramer, Robert M. Lipp, Lloyd A. Lippman, Henry Lloyd, Philip Machnikoff, Robert Nagler, Tom Peters, Paul H. Rich, Mel Prussack, Gerald Schoenfeld, Seymour G. Siegel, Allen Skupp, Robert Slass, Michael Slotopolsky, Larry Vogel, Roger W. Vogel, Harry Walker, Robert M. Weiss, Lynne Weiss-Marshall, Rabbi Eugene

Wernick, Sharon Kuflik Witchel, all my WithumSmith+Brown partners, and *Bartlett's Familiar Quotations.*

Publishing a book requires a close collaboration between the author, editors, artists, and project managers. The staff at iUniverse has been an invaluable asset and I would like to particularly thank George E. Nedeff, Lacey Perry, the unnamed line editor, Elaine Ward, John Maness, and the entire production staff for their responsive diligence in shepherding my initial manuscript into a finished book.

Special thanks to Don Gabor, coach extraordinaire, whose help and guidance led me to better organize and shape the book and make it much more concise.

Peter Weitsen who has been my partner, close friend, collaborator and continuous sounding board for over twenty years.

My parents—Ellen and Arthur Mendlowitz, may they rest in peace, who gave me the encouragement to do as much of what I could dream.

My clients who pushed me to excel.

Most of this book was written from notes and thoughts I accumulated throughout the years, going back to ideas I've gotten, and impressions I've formed, when I was quite young. Where applicable, I've attributed the idea or thought to the proper source. If I haven't, then it is an oversight, with the attribution being lost to me. I will gladly correct any oversights in the future if you would be kind enough to let me know which omission I have made.

All management and leadership books are work in progress. Readers are welcome to e-mail me their comments and questions at emendlowitz@withum.com and to check my website for additions and further information at www.edwardmendlowitz.com.

INTRODUCTION

As a CPA, I frequently am asked for help by busy clients who want management, leadership, and lifestyle information and advice quickly and focused. They don't want to waste time on something they can't process and apply immediately. To best serve them, I developed methods to communicate clearly and effectively and to become efficient with my use of words and their delivery. That is what I am sharing with you in this book.

Power Bites contains short sayings, brief explanations, and even shorter calls to action, but it is based on my long history of dealing with people who have shared their most important concerns about the strengths and weaknesses of their business— its future growth and viability, their comfort and security, their fears about being alone in the business even if they employ hundreds of people, and what keeps them awake at night.

I have been fortunate to work with many different kinds of successful businesspeople and executives, and *Power Bites* is a synthesis of that experience, inquisitiveness, and interest in thousands of clients and their problems. My role as their CPA has placed me in a unique position to offer you tested information in an easy-to-read, digest, and act on manner. Transferring and applying my experience quickly and succinctly is what I do, and it is what I have done in *Power Bites*. After you read this book and put its ideas into practice, I guarantee you a better night's sleep!

PART I
Self-Management

CHAPTER 1
Knowledge Creates Power

Knowledge creates power. Therefore, acquiring knowledge will give you power and make you perform better.

The more you know, the greater advantage you will have over those you work with ... and against.

Learn from the experiences of others. Don't rewrite the Bible. If someone has already found a solution, why should you try to find it by yourself when all you have to do is find out what they did? The amount of time will be a lot less than it will be for you to do what has already been done. Seek out business and industry leaders. Read their interviews, articles, and books, attend their speeches and podcasts, and become more aware of what is out there. Spend some time at least monthly looking at the new books in the bookstores or local public library; see what new magazines are being published and what types of articles they are publishing. It is also easy to do both of these at most airports.

It is impossible to know everything, to be able to learn everything, or to even know everything you should learn about. What you can do, however, is to never pass up an opportunity to learn something. On your journey through life you will come upon many new things. At that moment, use it as the time that you will learn about that item. When it comes to acquiring knowledge, the least you can do is not kick aside something you are tripping over. If you don't seize that moment, not only may it never come again, but you might be expected to know it from that point forward. And then you will never ever be able to learn it because, "Who could you ask?"

Just as knowledge creates power, so does information. Keep informed. Keep current. Read newspapers daily. And read the right newspapers. You should read a local daily paper. And, you should read a national daily paper, such as *The Wall Street Journal* or *New York Times*. And, it should be read before you enter the office in the morning, not at home at night after work.

Also, get into the habit of calling people or dropping notes to those you know that are mentioned in the news or if you read something that may be of interest to them. This helps them think of you as a resource or renews old acquaintances.

Access to knowledge and information also creates power. Know where you can get things answered and done. Keep an extensive reference library close by. Learn to effectively search the Web. Know whom to call. Become the person called by those you know. You may not know the answers for them, but you will learn what is important to them, and that will lead you to more knowledge. And then get them their answer!

CHAPTER 2
There Is No Acceptable Alternative to Growth

Learn new things. Don't ever stop learning.

Did you ever find that just when you think you know everything about a subject, you learn something new?

We are always learning. But how often do you go out of your way to learn?

Most of us learned how to read when we were about five or six years old. Did it ever occur to you that there might be a better way to read? You are following the same techniques you acquired when you were five. Why not investigate to see if there are new or better ways? Why not take a speed-reading course? It's fairly inexpensive and easy to bear, and it doesn't take up that much time. If you use the computer fairly often and can't touch type, why not learn? If you work with people whose native language is not English, why not learn their language?

When was the last time you took a course on anything? Why not now?

Learning and growth should be synonymous. In order to learn you must be surrounded by people from whom you can learn. And that doesn't always mean people smarter than you. An employee once asked me how I learned new things. One way is actually by the questions employees ask me. Not the questions that substitute for them looking something up, but truly insightful questions. Queries about why something is done a particular way, or the reasoning behind the methods, or even why something is necessary, can lead to learning by forcing you to rethink something that, somewhere along the way, became too obvious to you.

I once asked someone in his late seventies why he spends so much time learning and doing new things. He replied, "It's harder to hit a moving target!"

I am generally surrounded by entrepreneurs, so I am sometimes surprised by the comments of people that indicate closure on their energies. I have found that people who work for large organizations usually know their retirement date many years in advance. I have also observed that as they approach that date [usually about four to six years earlier] their minds stop becoming active in the functions of bettering their position. They become settled in at what they are doing and bide their time until they get that gold watch. Entrepreneurs, on the other hand, always seem to be looking for that next deal, their next big score, or the next step for their business. They are more stimulating to be with because nothing ever stays the same, and the learning never takes a vacation or retires.

Following is an inscription on a card I tell new staff to carry and look at on their way home each workday:

Ask yourself at the end of each day:

"What did I learn today?"
"What did others learn from me?"

If you do not get good answers
to both questions,
then perhaps that job or the people
you work with are not for you.

When you stop learning, you die. When you stop growing, you die. The only thing that might be delayed is the putting your body into the coffin.

Learning new things should be fun; sometimes it can be an arduous process, but it requires a start. Any action that moves you closer to what you want to learn is positive and worthwhile.

CHAPTER 3
You Learn from Listening, Not Talking

If talking was more important than listening, you would have two mouths and one ear.

How can you learn anything when you are talking?

Human nature being what it is, the more you let someone else talk, the smarter you seem.

Be an active listener. A good listener can still control the conversation by well spaced interruptions and short key questions leading or directing the speaker.

Choose whom you want to listen to—avoid ramblers and those who just like to hear themselves speak.

Be a responsible listener. If you are with someone who is supposed to learn from you, and they don't let you talk but do all the talking, you'll lose out when they realize they spent "wasted" time (even though it is of their choosing). You will lose positioning as a resource for them. When you are with them, try to redirect the discussion into the matter at hand. It sometimes needs you to interrupt them. In situations when it really is impossible to redirect the chatterer, follow up the next day with telephone "responses" to questions or issues raised or to what should have been conveyed by you, so your role as the trusted provider of important information will remain intact.

CHAPTER 4
Seek an Absence of Aggravation

What causes aggravation?

- Certain people and types of people
- Regretting something you've said
- Always working under pressure
- Getting less than you expected
- An absence of chemistry

I am sure you can add many other things to this list. These are things that get me aggravated.

Aggravation carriers are people who blame you for things you cannot control while they do the things they can control wrong.

Also, just because something usually aggravates me doesn't mean it always will. Sometimes my mood is such that nothing can bother me; at other times, everything bothers me.

There are certain types of people that bother me. It is generally a sloppy, disorganized person that is usually his sloppiest and most disorganized when I am with him, waiting for something that was promised to me and is late. This is the person that causes me to get angry with myself, either for subjecting myself to dealing with that person in the first place or for resenting having been placed in a position where I depend upon him for something critical. Also, "sloppy and disorganized" refers not just to the person's physical work, but to a way of thinking and reasoning. And the most aggravating part of all is that you can't even get that person to see why you are so mad. He always seems to be oblivious to your anger.

Saying things about people who are not present, and then being afraid they will find out what you said, creates a lot of undue anxiety for me. I know it will be repeated to them completely out of context, so there is no way I could ever rationalize what I said, even if I were given that opportunity! The simple solution to this is to never, *never*, ever say anything derogatory about someone who isn't present, and if he or she is present, never make those types of statements in public. This solution is a tremendous tension relaxer—and eliminates part of one of my aggravation triggers.

Working under pressure is necessary in business and in life. But to constantly work under pressure is sick. No amount of advance planning can cover every contingency. But lack of careful planning will take its toll on you and your organization. Plan things out and allow reasonable time for each to get done. If you need additional time, plan out overtime or hiring extra help or reassigning staff. Advance planning reduces the crisis atmosphere, tension level, and pressure. If you are constantly working under pressure, examine the reasons. Perhaps you are not delegating or assigning the work properly. Perhaps you are not supervising your staff properly, or often enough, or not giving them enough to do. Perhaps you are not scheduling the work with a proper amount of lead time or are not allowing for problems that might develop. Perhaps you are not being realistic about how long the job will take or are promising too-early delivery dates to oversatisfy a customer or client, when what the client needs is a due date they can rely on—a "money in the bank!" due date.

If you constantly are not getting what you want, you can alter this by reducing your expectations (shame on you!), or by making it crystal clear what you want and that nothing less will be accepted. This will take patience, perhaps a written note or memo, and a clear understanding by the person doing the work of what is acceptable and what a successful completion of the job is. It takes willingness on your part to acquire, monitor, and discuss updates while the job is being done and to refuse to accept work that is not complete. You must develop a tolerance to allow for screw ups and just plain aberrations from normal work practices. But you must not accept the job until it is the way it is supposed to be. If you need it by a certain date, then the responsibility is yours to check frequently on the progress to ensure it will be ready when you need it.

Take nice over smart. I want smart and nice people working for me. I don't want to have to choose between the two, but if I have to, I'll take nice every time, in every situation.

Everything works better if there is chemistry. Look for the chemistry in your relationships. If it doesn't feel right, it probably won't be right. The chemistry won't be there in everything you do, or with everyone you do something with, so you will have to make the best of those situations until you can extricate yourself from them.

Lots of times, in baseball, basketball, and other professional sports, a player doesn't seem to play at his potential and is traded to another team, where he blossoms. Why? He is the same person, but something has changed. What? It could have been the manager or coach, new teammates, the location or city, or simply that he is closer to home. Whatever the reason, it is the change to a positive chemistry.

In many cases you can look to create your own positive chemistry, or take the first step toward that goal. John Milton wrote in *Paradise Lost*, "The mind is its own place, and in itself, can make a heaven of hell, or a hell of heaven." Don't let your mind create the negative things. Have it focus on the positives. Don't let the other person's negative attitudes get you down or hold you back and override your positive feelings.

CHAPTER 5
Don't Lose Your Temper

Losing your temper will never accomplish anything. And it most likely will obstruct your getting what you want or need. Very few people can work effectively if they are the subject of an uncontrolled tirade. So you end up with a worse situation by losing your temper.

Most of the people I know that lose their temper think it shows how important they are since, if they are the boss, the subject of their anger doesn't talk back. Usually the subject can't or is afraid to, and their silence signifies, to their boss, consent to their nonsensical rambling.

I question the professional judgment of someone who loses their temper in a business setting. I can see where a parent might lose their temper at home if their four-year-old child plays post office and uses the stamps from a gold-medal stamp collection. But it mustn't happen in business, where you are only as effective as your backup staff allows you to be.

What can cause you to lose control in a business matter? If it is an isolated instance, it has to be overlooked. If it is because of repetitive, unacceptable performance, then the person to get mad at is yourself for not properly supervising the job or for self-directed exasperation or frustration due to your permitting or overlooking continual nonperformance or poor performance. Think how funny you will look yelling at yourself.

If you feel you can't discharge the source of your anger because you need that person where he or she is so the applecart won't be upset, then either that person is more valuable than you think or you are a fool. In either case, you must control your emotions and remain calm so that you can get the best that person has to offer, which is the reason that the person was hired in the first place.

Losing your temper is an ego trip nobody needs to be on in business. Consider the reaction of the person to whom it's directed. Can that person continue being as effective afterwards as he or she was before? You might feel a little better because you let off steam, but that small relief will haunt you later on because of a deteriorated relationship or diminished performance. Losing your temper will cause you to mortgage your future with that person and perhaps with others in earshot of the incident, and you will continually pay for it. Mortgaging your future occurs when you take advantage of a near term benefit that causes a greater long term detriment to you.

Yelling or arguing are not the only ways that show you lost your temper. Any loss of control can show a loss of temper. An example is when you are sarcastic or make funny faces. There is no reason to belittle someone and try to hurt their self-respect. You will never accomplish your objectives that way. And that is the ultimate goal—getting what you want. Very few will ever react positively and with excitement and enthusiasm to someone who puts them down. Also, complaining to someone over the telephone when the listener is in a room full of clients or customers or staff people, and where he or she can't respond or even let on what the conversation is about, creates an unfair situation that will never help you accomplish your objectives. If you are trying to let off steam so you will feel better, forget it. You will definitely feel worse in the long run, when you fall short of your objectives because there is no team behind you. And if you are trying to score points, who is counting? Isn't the person with the best-functioning team the winner? Points don't count in the real world.

Don't hold grudges. Life is too short to waste on arbitrary thought.

Don't spend energy on unproductive purchases. Go forward. Don't look back. Everything evens out at the end anyway.

Patience really is a virtue. Patience is the willingness to wait for something. Expecting something and not getting it on time can cause consternation. Have some fallback positions so you don't get angry. Try to understand why it was or will be late. Don't get me wrong, understanding is not forgiveness or condoning the situation. But it can help you through a period where you might lose your temper. Everything has a reason. They could be bad reasons as far as you are concerned, but they are reasons.

CHAPTER 6
Know Who You Are

You must know who you are. You must remember where you came from. If you don't show respect for your roots, others will lose respect for you.

Part of knowing who you are requires you to not hide it. Even if you don't want to flaunt it, you must not go out of your way to hide it, or deny it, or give the appearance that you are trying to cover it up or are embarrassed about it. Others judge you by the way you judge yourself. If you've ever heard a superconfident speaker, you probably felt good about being there because the speaker would have confirmed your good judgment in spending time with him/her, because that speaker is the best. On the other hand, a bad or less confident speaker gives you the distinct feeling that you've made a mistake. The tone is determined by the speaker's feelings about himself or herself.

We all want to show some individuality. In a business setting it is not that hard, although it is also not a piece of cake. The tie or scarf you wear sets a tone. Your shoe style or type of designer suit or lack of a tie tells someone who you are. How you furnish your office, dispose of your mail, or maintain your files or desktop sets a tone. Your choice of prints, posters, or art, or lack of it, also sends a message.

Nowadays in large firms you meet with someone who never lets you past the first conference room in their office suite. When that happens to me, I never quite get a true feel for that person. We do our business, but it's hard for me to get the "personality" of who I am interacting with. I like to see their personal work space. Nowadays you can search them and their personal pages out on the Web. See what they write about themselves and the kind of messages and remarks they make. See who their friends or contacts are. Use what you have at your disposal to "get" their personalities. Linkedin, Facebook and MySpace replaced the knick knacks on the desk and photos and posters on the office walls and are the new ways to size up someone's personality.

Writing a personal and company mission statement helps define who you are and what you are about. You don't have to publish it, but you should write it down. If you try it, I think you will be surprised at how difficult it is to do. But it will give you a much clearer idea about who you are and a much greater ability to communicate it to those around you.

Confident people surround themselves with talented, gifted, intelligent, strong-minded people. Weak people don't. Look at the people around you and around those you do business with.

Know your role. It is not so easy. In *Megatrends*, John

Nesbitt points out that the railroads, at the turn of the century, envisioned themselves as being in the railroad business and not the transportation business. When trucks and planes came about, train companies missed a business growth opportunity. The big CPA firms do not think of themselves as CPAs, but as information providers and business advisers. That is why they are among the largest management and computer consultants in the world today. If they had only stuck to audits, they would have lost a great opportunity. Is the job of a CPA to do tax returns and audits, or to provide information the client won't ordinarily get? The legal profession abandoned the practice of tax return preparation to the accountants. And the professional accountants are abandoning the low-end tax preparation business to the H&R Block-type firms, and them to Turbo Tax® and other software producers.

Around 1993 it appeared that IBM did not understand its role. The company thought it had a lock on the computer business. That might have been true with regard to certain types and sizes of computers. But the marketplace started to abandon that end of the business about a dozen years earlier, and IBM, either through arrogance, ignorance, stubbornness, or just plain "head-in-the-sand" syndrome, lost its dominance. Major realignment seems to have reversed that, and they are in a different business today—in a market-domineering style. However, there are many examples of almost monopolistic companies that no longer exist because they did not recognize their role. Make it your business to know yours.

Since I am a CPA, I think a lot about the role of CPAs. Sometimes I wake up and think about what would happen to CPAs if there was a worldwide prolonged depression with everyone fighting for survival. Would CPAs still be engaged to tell clients their net worth, or would they be retained to help clients better employ their resources during the depression? This latter information would be well worth the CPA's fee, because the knowledge gained and monies saved or made would be far more than the CPA's fee, while the former information might not serve any useful purpose—the client not hiring the CPA might not know their net worth, but they would know that whatever it is, it is higher than it would be had they paid the CPA to know! CPAs are a perfect example of a profession that has recognized its role. The accounting profession, more than any other, has changed with the times. The role of a CPA today is not necessarily what it was just ten years ago, and certainly not what it was twenty years ago, and, I might suggest, not what it will be ten years from now. The CPA's role is unique in that it is the closest, objective-minded, independent adviser to business owners and managers. And CPAs have taken note and advantage of that role by becoming among the largest nonpublicly held companies in the world.

A paradox in roles is the auto industry. The auto manufacturers sell "retail" to their dealers, who then sell "wholesale" to the public. Think about that. The selling model hasn't changed in the auto industry since the 1930s, even with the information-laden Internet. Another is in the department store industry, where many items are sold at "full" price for only a short enough time to establish the regular retail price, and then the discounts and markdowns start. The Wal-Marts and Home Depots made changes, but not such revolutionary changes as other businesses. Actually, a major competitive edge of Wal-Mart is its computerized distribution system that keep costs down, and that is what it passes on to its customers.

In the mid-1990s, Newt Gingrich fully understood the role of the Republican minority when he formulated the "Contract with America." He defined clearly the difference between the Republicans and the Democrats. He understood his role at that time. And he was able to articulate it clearly and succinctly. That gave the voters something to vote for. However, I don't think anyone else followed to even copy him, let alone move his political methodology forward. In 2008, Barack Obama clearly defined his differences with Hillary Clinton and then with John McCain to capture the minds of voters and cause a "revolution" by the electorate.

There are some managers I know that are great at fixing and solving problems—seeing them in action is a thing of beauty. However, some of these same people have no ability to anticipate a problem—either because they don't view it as important (possibly because it hasn't yet occurred), or as being their job, or through an inability to conceptualize what might or can happen. These people should be placed in managerial positions of the highest order, but not leadership positions, where a solid vision needs to be offered and implemented. You might say this is a difference between what makes a manager and what makes a leader.

An ancient Greek said it best: "Know thyself."[1]

---

1   Attributed to The Seven Sages, c. 600 BCE. – Thales, Solon, Periander, Cleobulus, Chilon, Bias and Pittacus. Inscription from the Delphic Oracle, From Plutarch, Morals. Also attributed to others, but they were all Greek.

CHAPTER 7
Focus In on Every Client, Issue, or Matter

What you do, you do. Who you do it for needs it, and they need it right and as perfect as possible, and on time.

Don't shortchange your customers, clients, or staff by not paying attention or focusing in on what you are doing. "Focusing in" means that you give the matter at hand your complete, undivided attention. You concentrate on it. You think about it. You analyze it. You make sure it's done right. You make sure it's done as well as it can be done. You make sure you cover every angle and find every loophole. You make sure it is acceptable by the highest standards. You treat it as if it is the single most important thing you ever have to do, because the customer or client will apply that feeling when he or she receives and reviews what you are doing.

One of my clients once told me that he was using my firm primarily because of my creative abilities. He continued by saying that he would get full value of that if, once every three months, I would close my office door, hold my telephone calls, and do nothing but think about what I could do for him. He felt confident that if I did that, I would come up with enough game-winning home runs for him to get more value than what he was paying for. I now do this at least quarterly for every client, project, and activity in which I am involved. And it works!

People who engage you to do something do so because they not only think you will do it well, but that you will treat it with proper care and will look out for their best interests. Don't neglect your job by having your mind on other matters.

Think for a moment how you feel when you have stomach cramps. You feel terrible. Right? You feel like the cramps will never go away. Right? You wish the cramps would go away. Right? You don't want to bother with anything, or speak to anybody, or do anything. Right? Well, at this very moment while you are reading this, you don't have any cramps. Right? And are you grateful and appreciative that you don't have them? Probably not until you read this and are now fully aware that you don't have the cramps. However, you were feeling fine a few seconds ago but didn't pay any mind to it because you didn't focus in on it or pay attention to it, like you are right now. That's what I mean by focusing in. Give it your full concentration and thoughts.

IBM's slogan was "THINK!" What was the thinking when the decision was made in the 1970s to go ahead with a personal computer and to outsource the chip to Intel and the operating system to Microsoft? No one seemed to be focusing in on what was really going to happen.

I once saw a bumper sticker that said "Don't get too attached to your bumper sticker—the car might break down!" Be flexible in your thinking, and leave yourself room to maneuver. However, focus in carefully and fully on what you are doing.

The most successful people are those with a single idea, for which they fully exhaust every possibility. Many times if that idea is not successful, they then go on to the next idea. But they are deeply concentrating on one idea at a time. They are focused on the task at hand.

Focusing goes hand in hand with thoroughness. Don't give up without a fight. And don't give your work a 90 percent effort. Work painstakingly and completely at your trusted position.

The focus of a business is to make money by making its customers happy. Everything should strive toward that focus.

It's the petty things that rob us of our time, not the big things. You must arm yourself against the small minds of people who refuse to focus in on the issues at hand. Examples abound at meetings, but it also happens in one-on-one confrontations. Ask yourself if what you are doing is what you are supposed to be doing at that moment.

PART II
Leadership

CHAPTER 8
Develop a Vision

Be a dreamer. Develop a vision. Set goals for your organization. The vision is the game plan for the future. Without it, there is no direction, motivation, or interest.

Learn to fantasize. Think of the absurd. Apply ideas from one industry to another. Analyze procedures. Break them down into easier tasks. Make them idiot-proof.

Share your vision. Promote it. Set the tone for it. Manage the values of your organization and measure them against your vision.

Visions should deal with big-picture items; otherwise, you will waste your energy. Visions are the maps that lead to creativity and accomplishment.

Big-picture items are difficult to conceptualize, introduce, focus, and press forward on, and take time to see positive changes. Small-picture items fall into a comfort zone of achievement but don't cause major business growth changes.

Visions do not have to be realistic. How realistic was the telephone, air travel, the radio, atomic energy, and the Internet? But they do have to result in some eventual benefit.

George Washington, John Adams, and Thomas Jefferson, among many others, had a vision that, at the time, was extremely unrealistic. Bill Gates had a vision, also unrealistic. So did the creators of Starbucks, McDonald's, and Disney World. And, actually, so did Warren Buffett!

Once you have that vision, translate it into a goal, and the goal into a course of action. And do not let any skeptics dissuade you or divert you from your road. Do not compromise your vision if it pushes you off track. Compromises in details might be necessary to build a consensus, but only allow them if the main vision is not altered.

President Reagan had a vision of a better America, and he condensed it into a small number of things he wanted accomplished, such as a reformed tax code, a reversal of the high inflation he inherited, and the demise of the Soviet Union, and then he focused his energy on those items. His visions became his accomplishments. His successor did not seem to have as clear a vision and, accordingly, appeared to be unfocused (an exception was the war with Iraq). The same appeared to be the case with President Clinton's tenure.

People need to know their leaders have a vision. They do not have to agree with it, but they need to know that their leaders know where they would like to go. The vision translates into a clear focus, which provides a feeling of confidence—usually.

Visions are associated with future change, but they don't necessarily need to be. A simple vision for a troubled company could be to become profitable and provide job security for the company's employees, customers, and suppliers.

A leader needs to decide what type of leader he or she wants to be—a reactor or someone who drives the business and its profits forward

A vision is a company's central direction, its identity, its focus.

CHAPTER 9
Set Goals

I wrote this chapter and the previous one at different times, and when I organized the book it seemed that goals and visions are similar, if not the same. So what is the difference? It seems that visions are the big-picture successes a company wants to achieve. Goals are the means of setting up the steps that get you there. Either way, or whatever they're called, you should have both of them.

Goals are the road maps that take you there. If you have the right maps, you'll have a much better chance of getting where you want to go, and sooner and more easily. The same thing applies to goals.

Goals create a direction for you. They also set a path that you can use to see if it is realistic. Sometimes we set goals that are too ambitious and unrealistic. It is not bad to dream, but it is counterproductive to set something so difficult to achieve that you have no sensible hope of completing it. What I suggest is that you set a major goal and then set a series of smaller goals or benchmarks that will take you closer to where you want to be. Then concentrate on the immediate smaller goals.

After you set your goals you should determine how what you are doing will bring you closer to those goals. The goals also can serve as motivators to help you work toward them. Having a purpose will make the task easier and more attainable.

If you are a leader, where do you want to go? People will generally (or at least for some period or time, if not forever) follow their leader. Are you setting the right path for them to follow?

Children will follow the values of their parents. But they may not be the values the parents want their children to follow. Watch the way you act, and match them to your goals.

Set goals in everything you do. You can have multiple goals. Just try to limit your energy to big-picture items.

An example of a long term goal is to have financial security when it is time for you to retire. A current goal could be to save a little each week or paycheck. Not saving anything or living beyond your means is spending tomorrow's earnings eventually thwarting your long term goal. Is this what you really want to do?

A goal sets the direction in which you travel. Once set, you should measure whether you are going toward or away from your goal. Determine your efforts by how much closer they bring you to your goals.

You can use goals to keep you set on the big picture. Looking at and memorizing details may make you knowledgeable about a subject, but synthesizing and applying the information will make you more effective.

New year's resolutions are statements of goals. Do you find yourself repeating the same resolutions year after year? If so, then it is time to take some action and either follow the resolution or set easier goals. This could be similar to the little girl who asks her father why he has to take work home every night instead of being put in a slower group. Set realistic goals, and then "do it!"

Don't end up with a long list of "wish I hads." I wish I had gone to Venice; I wish I had learned to play the piano; I wish I had learned French; I wish I had ...

Setting goals is a way to create balance in your life. You have to balance making a living with caring for your family and pursuing personal interests.

I know some people who are very successful today. I knew them when they were first starting their business careers. They had a very narrowly directed goal—to become a "player." How they became that, and in what fields, is not important. What is important is their single-minded determination to become a player. Everything they did had to take them to that goal, or it was dropped. They were fortunate enough, and perhaps lucky enough, to attain their goals. But it was with very hard work directing them solely to their goals.

Time has to be balanced between the long-range "big-picture" goals, and the shorter-range daily tasks we must do. Too often we forget the big picture altogether. Don't!

CHAPTER 10
Follow Through on Your Projects

Try to be the person who comes up with the ideas. Better yet, be the person who follows through with the ideas. No matter who comes up with the ideas, nothing can happen unless someone makes it happen.

The person doing the work and the follow-through will control the project. If you don't think this is so, think about the last project you assigned to someone. Was it done when you wanted it, and how you wanted it? Or did that person decide how and when it was to get done?

Stalling and procrastinating are methods by which decisions not to proceed are made. They are methods designed to avoid making decisions. Are you going to run your life by default decisions?

Think of all your lost opportunities because you didn't follow through. Resolve right now not to let any more lost opportunities hold you back. I think John Greenleaf Whittier[2] said it best:

> For of all sad words of tongue or pen,
> The saddest are these: "It might have been!"

Calvin Coolidge, a man known for few words, put it in complete perspective with the following words:

Press On

Nothing in the world can take the place of persistence.
Talent will not; nothing is more common than unsuccessful men with talent.
Genius will not; unrewarded genius is almost a proverb.
Education will not; the world is full of educated derelicts.
Persistence and determination alone are omnipotent.
The slogan "Press On" has solved and always will solve the problems of the human race.

Occasionally it is faster to do it the long way. Shortcuts usually don't help, and the work can end up being redone. Do not sidestep procedures. If the project has to be redone, it almost ensures that you will have to start from the beginning. Also, if you did it the "long way," others can usually pick up where you left off.

2   Poem: Maud Muller

CHAPTER 11
Prepare for Surprises

Nothing beats being prepared. Preparing for all contingencies keeps you alert to surprises.

The way you prepare is subject to the possibilities that are probable. You don't, and shouldn't, have to over prepare for eventualities that stretch the mind—unless that is what you're trying to accomplish with your client/customer/boss/etc. And what's wrong with trying to do that?

Be prepared. Why is it that the person you are least prepared for always calls when you are at your busiest? Why do you always run out of fresh batteries when you want to dictate something while you are stuck somewhere waiting for someone, or why does the smoke detector set off a "replace battery" beep as soon as you arrive at your destination, and you call your wife to tell her you've arrived?

Did you ever want to use a key that you didn't have with you? Why not carry an unmarked duplicate set of keys in the trunk of your car or your briefcase or in whatever you always carry or bring with you?

Try to imagine a carpenter with a full toolbox, with every gadget he could possibly need, except that he is short a Phillips head screwdriver. Now put your business in that place. Are you constantly short that one screwdriver?

Plan ahead. We all know we should plan ahead. But we usually don't. The successful people do plan ahead. Don't you want to be successful?

Always have a fallback position. If you know where you are going, you can anticipate not getting there. What will happen? Plan for it, and it will be much easier to deal with.

It is amazing what you can accomplish if you plan in advance. Cities are built one brick at a time. Plan your steps, and it will be much easier for you to visualize the completed project.

Small things done on a repetitive basis can accomplish much or can cause great damage. A student's regular studying gives him/her command of the lessons. A small continuous leak in the ceiling of a building can destroy the building. The leak causes a very small portion of the facade to wear away. In the winter the water inside the wall turns to ice. The ice expands and causes a much bigger hole. The bigger hole allows more water to get inside, until, during a fierce storm, the wall or roof caves in, causing a terrible flood inside the building. (I know this is so. I used to own an apartment building, and one of the tenants didn't get around to telling me about the leak.)

Expect irrational behavior. Everything we learn and everywhere we learn teaches us what is rational, how to be rational, and how to deal with the rational. But it's dealing with the irrational that makes us who and what we are, and determines our course of action. I don't like it, but it is so.

Expect it. Deal with it. And be surprised (and glad) when you don't encounter it.

But, alas, there are exceptions. Nothing could have prepared us for the terrible events of September 11, 2001.

Stuff happens. So-called "conventional wisdom" sometimes doesn't allow for unexpected results—the Titanic, the Edsel, Enron, Lehman Brothers, BearStearns, AIG, Merrill Lynch, Chrysler, Washington Mutual.

Normal uncertainties include planes being late, disconnected conference calls, electrical surges, death, tax changes, inane news reports interrupting the last ten minutes of a season-ending TV soap, or being invited on the same day to a one-hundredth birthday party, a wedding, and the seventh game of the World Series.

CHAPTER 12
Don't Be Afraid to Try Something New

If you don't try, how can you succeed? And if you try, you will make mistakes. So what? Would you be better off if you never tried? Most likely not! So, do. And make mistakes along the way. It is the way to grow and accomplish.

Be in the ball game. Be a player. There are two types of people who buy lottery tickets—those who check the numbers and those who don't. Otherwise, how can you account for the large number of winning tickets that remain unclaimed?

Participate. Be active. Get involved. Take your licks.

I know many people who failed successively in business only to finally succeed. They were determined to win. The losses were only the warm-ups. The real game, the Super Bowl of life, was the winning entry. The times the ball was carried created the skills needed to win. Don't sit on the sidelines, unless that is what you really like.

Babe Ruth hit 714 home runs, and struck out 1,330 times. His total plate appearances were 10,504, so he struck out about 13 percent of the time. He was also out 4,196 other times. He failed more times than he succeeded in his plate appearances. Would he have been better off by being less aggressive—by playing more cautiously or less often? (By the way, Ruth gets my vote as being the best baseball player of all time. Besides being a .342 lifetime batter, as a pitcher in 163 games his won-lost percentage was .671 and his earned run average was 2.28. These pitching statistics would put him in the top ten if he had enough decisions to be considered a career pitcher. He also pitched 107 complete games out of 148 games he started—72 percent. Today, a complete game merits a headline!)

Quash fears. The worst thing hindering creativity is the fear of failing. Fears set limits. Don't limit yourself. Expand your mind as far as it can take you.

Creativity can be encouraged. It may not be learned, but it can be taught. One technique I used with my children when they were very young was to bring home reams of copy machine paper and give it to them to color and draw on. This enabled them to be creative. They had no choice. The paper and crayons were there for the taking by them. They didn't know they were being creative; they were just having fun. If they didn't like something, they just threw it away and started again with another blank sheet. Now contrast this to the child that gets a coloring book with heavy lines setting boundaries for their coloring and a parent who chastises them because the work is not neat enough. Who will be the creative one? Sometimes I see the very neat colorers in business settings, and notice the blinders they use as they travel around life, never through life, just around it. It is a pity.

Big-picture mistakes. Big picture focus means big-picture mistakes. The biggest risks give the biggest gains ... and losses. When you are the boss, go for it. Just try to break the project into segments so that the losses can be somewhat contained.

Ready, fire, aim. Do things. Get started. Experiment. Stop talking and planning and thinking and conjecturing. Do it! The worst that can happen is that it doesn't work. "Ready, fire, aim" has been attributed to so many people I don't know who to attribute it to, but it works! Note: I am referring to new and creative endeavors. For your regular work you had better plan and think about it. I have noticed that when plans are made in a committee no one starts acting on them until they are told to "go!" The "go" is held up (remember, it is a committee) until all the i's are dotted and the t's are crossed, and the brochures are printed, and sales and back office staffs prepped. Why can't the people in the meeting just get started individually once they realize it is a good idea?

Oh—always spell check! Find your own errors. Don't sign off on a job where you didn't check for *your* errors. We all make mistakes. The better performers just find the time to check for their own mistakes. Most tasks have self-checking mechanisms. Find them and use them!

CHAPTER 13
Admit Mistakes

Everyone makes mistakes. The problems build up if you continually make mistakes and don't learn from previous ones.

The problems also grow when you deny you made a mistake when you are caught red-handed. No one can fault an error. It's the denial or stupid excuses that upset people.

When you are confronted with an error you made, 'fess up to it immediately. If you can, explain why the mistake was made. Apologize profusely and tell them it won't—can't—happen again … and why it won't reoccur. And correct it immediately! And graciously!

If someone under you makes a mistake, apologize as if you made the mistake. You did! You didn't supervise your subordinate properly.

Note: What should you do if you've discovered your error?

Don't air dirty laundry in public. Your faults and the faults of your associates are no one else's business—if you want to remain in business. Don't ever complain or discuss negative thoughts about those with whom you work. If you have to reprimand someone, do it when no one else is present. It can never help you to do it publicly. Never!

If you spend time bringing your staff, subordinates, and associates down, you are not leaving too much room for them to boost you up. In most instances, you will always be slightly above your subordinates. If your subordinates are pushed down, so will you be. But, placing them on a high pedestal will elevate you higher than you could ever do for yourself.

CHAPTER 14
Don't Close Your Eyes to the Obvious

Sometimes the simplest solution is the best.

Look at the project. Understand it. And then get it done as simply as possible.

One method I use is to periodically perform many of the procedures and functions that are done in my office. I am not looking for loads of work, so I usually choose a part of a project that is not voluminous. For example, if I want to test the procedures the tax administrator is following when she assembles tax returns, I'll choose a small one to do, and then I'll actually assemble it. In doing the one return, I get to test all the procedures that are followed. Some of the things I particularly care about are that all the procedures are followed uniformly and that the instructions are easy to follow and easy to use for training others. I am also looking for ways to streamline the system. I feel it can only be effectively done if I "get my hands dirty" once in a while. A manager can't be effective and set up systems if he never gets up from his desk.

When confronted with an overcrowded closet, remember that there is always a hanger on the floor.

When using your computer, if you set it to automatically put the current date on what you are doing, you lose the ability to know when it was originally done.

It takes longer to back into a parking spot than to back out.

A good method is to make sure you understand the task at hand before starting—and making sure your associates fully understand what they are to do before they start.

CHAPTER 15
Create Excitement!

People working for you should eagerly look forward to coming to work every day. They should go home bursting with ideas they want to try tomorrow. They should spread the word about the great company where they work. Their children should want to follow in their footsteps. Their friends should be a little (just a little) envious.

Life is too short to not enjoy all of it. And working is about half of your waking life.

President Kennedy comes to mind when I think of someone who created excitement. His youthful good looks, energy and exuberance, passion and intensity, hope and anticipation, wrapped together with all his mannerisms, couldn't help but create excitement. Even today, looking at old film clips brings, to me, an air of excitement. The person who can capture that energy will have a charged field of excitement surrounding everything he or she does.

One time, in my NYC practice, I had a partners' meeting scheduled and was looking for something to change the complacent mood that seemed to settle in among the staff. They had to be constantly motivated and made to feel that not only were we the best firm to work for, but they should deem it an honor and privilege. And this was in a time when it was (it still is) a sellers' market for CPA firm staff! I devoted the agenda to figuring out how to create excitement. I had signs made and placed in the meeting room that said, "Create Excitement!" The signs appeared to set a tone, and my partners eagerly devoured the topic. Needless to say, the meeting was successful, and the ideas propelled our firm to greater heights—with an extremely enthused staff spreading the word.[3]

Inspire and motivate, and you will create excitement. Have your people constantly learn new things, and they will be excited.

Action and speed create excitement. Doing something that appears, and hopefully will be, positive and innovative brings energy to your team members. Communicate what you are doing. Market to your employees the same way you would market to new clients. The enthusiasm of your personnel will translate into higher productivity, lower turnover, and a more secure base.

Everything needs excitement to succeed and sustain itself. Baseball needed a Babe Ruth. Boxing a Muhammad Ali,

---

3   Readers can check out my award-winning article in the March 2001 issue of the *Journal of Accountancy*, "Nine Ways to Make Your Firm More Exciting.". Go to: http://www.journalofaccountancy.com/Issues/2001/Mar/NineWaysToMakeYourFirmMoreExciting

basketball a Michael Jordan, the Great Depression of the early 1930s a Franklin Delano Roosevelt. America in 1981 needed the optimism and patriotism of a Ronald Reagan, and in 2009 it needed the energy and promise of change of Barack Obama.

Create a dramatic center. Establish a focal point for attention, action, and direction. People work better when they are directed toward an end or goal. This by itself creates excitement as long as there is forward movement. The more positive the forward movement, the more excitement there is.

CHAPTER 16
Think Positively

Be an optimist. Look for the good in everything. Consider that the bad in something is the cost of the good. Everything has a price. Be prepared to pay it. There are no free rides.

Be realistic about your goals, but don't set goals that are too easy to attain.

Only reaching for stars that you can touch is setting your sights too low, and you will sell yourself short. It is okay to dream and fantasize and to set "reach" goals—and then try for some of them! Balance your dreams with your capabilities.

When Benjamin Franklin[4] was a young businessman, he recognized that he had some shortcomings. He was able to define and categorize them into thirteen attributes. He then set a goal of trying to improve each one for a week at a time. In the course of a year, he would cover each area four times. Two

---

4   *Autobiography of Benjamin Franklin*, available in *every* bookstore in the United States.

things can be learned from this. One, set your sights high and reach for them. Two, break down a project into small portions so that the task could be managed more easily. Taken as a whole, it was an overwhelming job. As smaller parts, it was easily obtainable with focused attention. Conclusion: based upon Franklin's accomplishments, his reach and process seemed to be quite successful.

A number of years ago I started doing push-ups. My goal was to do ten, and it took quite a while to get to that number comfortably. Then twelve. Then fifteen. Then I realized I set my goal too low. Each time I set a new level, it was a struggle to reach it. I then set my goal at twice what I was doing at the time, which was, I believe, thirty. Somehow it became easier to get up to twenty-seven or twenty-eight than it was to get to twelve or fifteen. Set your sights on what is attainable and reach for it with stark determination. It works!

Setting your goals too short will leave you shortchanged. Many people set goals and then stop when they reach them. The superstars constantly set new goals and then newer ones. They never rest on their laurels.

Always move toward your goals. "A journey of a thousand miles starts with a single step." (Lao-Tzu)

CHAPTER 17
Smile

Nobody likes a grouch!

How many times do you get served by a waiter or waitress with a frown or with a smile that is nowhere close to being cheerful? Doesn't that shape your opinion of that restaurant? Your goodwill efforts with customers, employees, suppliers, and even the general public can be doomed to failure by the lack of a smile or a cheerful look. The success of the Walt Disney theme parks is, in part, due to the cheerful smiles of *all* their personnel (cast members), and to their eager willingness to help, to make sure you have a pleasant visit.

The attitude of an organization can be determined by the mood of those in charge, perhaps the single person at the top. If he or she comes in one morning or returns from lunch angry, brusque, or short-tempered, that can set the tone for everyone seeing this person for the rest of the day and even the next few days, until the boss changes their mood or a positive mood change is evident. The person at the top of the ladder is the cheerleader. Don't ever forget that! No one could ever say President Reagan wasn't a merry optimist and a happy cheerleader! He helped change our country's mood after the glum days of his predecessor.

Don't be a bore. Don't engage in idle, inane chatter. Don't show people the thirty-six, seventy-two, or, ugh, 108 baby pictures you took last weekend. Don't talk about the things you don't want to hear from others.

A bore is someone who, when you ask how they are, they tell you.[5]

Being a grouch is contagious—so is smiling.

---

5   Bert Leston Taylor, writing in *The So-Called Human Race.*

CHAPTER 18
Never Lie

Your boss shows you her newly designed corporate logo that cost $182,000 to produce and asks your opinion about what you think of it. You really think it stinks. What do you say?

Your reputation is the most valuable thing you have when you deal with people. Building that reputation takes a lifetime. One false step can shatter it. You must protect it with everything you have. One fib, one falsehood, one sentence less than the complete truth in a volume of remarks, one slip, however unconscious, can doom that reputation. Scrupulously guard your reputation. Never lie!

Telling your boss that you think the new logo is very, very, very interesting is a fine way of getting out of what could be a very embarrassing situation—and is a factually correct statement! Perhaps the blunt truth is more appropriate—as long as it is said in private and framed as your "uninformed" opinion.

There is a credibility threshold for most people and things. At some point, if it is crossed, you can't get it back. This applies to governments and its leaders, parents and children, and in business situations. If you cross that threshold, you lose respect for yourself, for your company or organization, and for what you are trying to accomplish. If you have credibility, you don't have to be well liked to get your points across. If you don't have credibility, you can never be well liked, and you will never get your points across. You cross the threshold when you lie or hide or cover up the truth!

Someone lied to me when I was fourteen years old, and I never forgot it. A large and well-known stamp dealer offered, at a special guaranteed price if he received payment in advance, a set of stamps honoring the marriage of Grace Kelly to Prince Rainier. When the set was issued, he did not honor the price. I received a letter telling me the price would be higher. I don't remember what I did, but I remembered that the stamp dealer lied in his advertisements, and I never bought from him again. He claimed a reputation for integrity. I know differently!

CHAPTER 19
You Can't Cheat
an Honest Person

That was said by P. T. Barnum. He also said, "There is a sucker born every minute."

If you think about the people you know who were cheated in a deal, try to remember whether they were completely honest or whether they were trying to take unfair advantage of the other person or other people. Usually, they were also trying to get away with something.

One of my rules for this is: when there are two people trying to cheat each other, the one who spends the money gets beat.

When confronted with a deal too good to be true, it usually is. You can approach it honestly but "neglect" to do the proper due diligence because "you don't want to find something that could quash the deal" or are "afraid to show ingratitude for being allowed into the deal." The desire to get something "better" than everyone else can cloud what would be considered normal business judgment. Push the pencil and do the work, and if you cannot, then walk.

Sometimes no matter what you do and no matter how hard you try, you will get suckered. It happens! The only way to minimize this is to have a fair-minded view toward everything you do.

PART III
Delegating

CHAPTER 20
When Others Push the Pencil for You, Make Sure It's Your Pencil

Always supervise those to whom you delegate an important task.

If you are a manager, then manage. Learn to manage. Read about how to manage. Take courses. Listen to tapes or CDs or watch Webinars. Discuss your management style or techniques with your peers, superiors, friends, and outside consultants.

If you are a manager, don't get caught in the trap of doing the work or taking the responsibility for moving the job forward. Doing is a direct conflict with managing. You can only *do* one thing at a time, but you can manage, supervise, or train many projects at the same time.

William Oncken Jr.[6] wrote about the managing technique where you should think of the job at hand as a monkey that is

6   "Managing Management Time," article in *Harvard Business Review*, *1984*. See Book List at end of book for more references.

on the shoulders of the person who has to do the job. When a subordinate asks for help on a project and the boss says he will think about it, the monkey jumps from the shoulders of the subordinate onto the boss. At the end of the day, the subordinates' jobs are done. They have no open items—no monkeys. The boss, though, has the load of four, five, or six subordinates, who very carefully and diligently shed their monkeys from their shoulders onto that of their boss. The trick is not to end up with the monkey. I never let a staff person under me leave my office when I have to do something before the subordinate can proceed with his or her job. I do not let him or her give me their monkeys. If a decision needs to be made by me, I ask my team member to lay out two or three alternatives so I can pick the best one. He or she leaves my office with a new assignment, and it is usually one that would help the employee develop further in his or her position!

Subordinates can't grow if they are not given responsibility, and if they are not put in a position where they could screw up. Don't put them where they could foul up a major project or lose a large order, but responsibility for a small part of the project won't be the end of the world. A proper manager/delegator has the decisions made and the work done at the lowest possible level.

No one is born with all the skills he or she will need. Help develop younger staff. Don't be greedy in passing on the skills you've acquired. Your skills in delegating will serve you by allowing you to move up to more valuable situations.

Training takes many forms. You can sit down and explain

why the job is being done or needs to be done. You can have the employee do something without your explaining the purpose, and when the job is finished, ask him or her to explain why it was done. You can recommend a book or course relevant to their work. You can take less experienced staff members to meetings to see how you do things.

Whatever your method, there should be a payback to you—a dividend. The dividend could be in the form of a comment or question about something you overlooked, the following up of additional work that has to be done, the training of someone else in the skill, teaching the boss something he or she didn't know, assumption of greater responsibilities, a more alert person, and a better overall product. If you do not notice the payback or dividend, then evaluate your training technique, your standards, and the performance and ability of the person you are trying to train. The trainee may be the wrong person. I use the dividend policy, and it hones me in rapidly to the general abilities of the people with whom I work. I expect frequent dividends from everyone I work with. A quick method to accumulate dividends, or to realize that the subordinate is not getting it, is when I take them to a meeting and there is no follow-up by them of any sort or no expression of interest. Another tip-off is when I am taking five times more notes than they are.

Understand what motivates people. I have found that people need three things from a job—money, opportunity, and satisfaction. People generally won't leave a job if two of the three are present. Any two! Many people won't leave a low-paying job if there is excellent opportunity and high job satisfaction.

Actually, the easiest one of the three is money—paying the right salary will reduce turnover.

I always try to have team members go home feeling they've done a great job that day. They must feel satisfied. Imagine if they were, and they walked into their homes and were asked by their children if they had a good day and they reply, "I had a great day!" Compare that to someone who feels all they were doing all day is punching a clock. He or she might reply, "Work stinks!" or "None of your business!" or some similar, harsh remark. The feelings emanating from employees about their jobs become the mirror image of how those around them view their work.

When you have to criticize someone, be quick, specific, and to the point. Don't expand the scope beyond the matter at hand. If the person's overall performance is poor or needs improvement, don't do it while you are telling him or her about a specific screw up. Do that as part of a formal job evaluation. Note that a formal evaluation doesn't need to be at fixed, scheduled times—it can be whenever it is considered necessary or appropriate.

It is also good to compliment freely. Compliments reinforce the efforts and certainly perk up the ego and future efforts. It never hurts to compliment someone in front of others. It always hurts to reprimand in front of others.

Entry-level or new staff must be made to understand that they need to fully comprehend any instructions given, that they are expected to ask plenty of questions and then do exactly what they are told to do. Every detail must be followed. If it isn't, they have to be reminded each and every time. A confidence level must be built up in that person, and that comes from the ability to follow instructions exactly. Also, it is imperative that your instructions be clear and not subject to misinterpretation.

Don't confuse sticking to details with micromanaging. They are used in two completely different disciplines. When you are training someone, that is the job at hand. The attention to details is part of that function. When dealing with the big picture of leading people or the business, the details should be left to others.

Don't let people working for you see you cut corners. That will become their new standard. Instead, let them see you pay attention to the details (and rules) when you are actually performing a task or function.

Measure people by how well they do what they are supposed to be doing, not by what you might want them to be doing but haven't told them yet.

Keep in mind that when training someone, he or she might be more interested in getting the job done than in understanding the entire history of how you got to this point in your life. My technique is to break the job at hand into small tasks that don't need more than a few words of instruction. No explanations. Just short instructions. After the employee has done the job a few times, he should understand why he is doing what he is doing. If he still doesn't, then he can ask me his questions. It is also easier to review a small job than a big job.

Create leverage. Delegate everything you can. If you always feel you can do it better and quicker and don't like taking the time to train someone, then you aren't management material.

Everything has some repetitive parts. Start with delegating that.

Learn the strengths and weaknesses of your staff. Then exploit their strengths and shield them from their weaknesses. Use each person to their fullest. Then each person does what he or she does best. Occasionally challenge an employee. If he or she accepts it, you've got a winner. And then push like crazy!

Many people are poor starters and finishers but are great in the middle. Most of the work is in the middle. Therefore, find ways to shorten the beginning and the end. This will lengthen the middle. Be prepared to give close assistance when the job starts and when it is about to end. Develop procedures to get people started quickly. In medias res is the way John Milton got the reader started with *Paradise Lost*. Get someone into the middle ASAP. Finishing up will need more help. Schedule yourself to be available at that point. Until the person has more experience, that is your job.

Have you ever been in a hospital? All the floors are the same, and they all have the same number of personnel. Yet, some floors are more organized and run much better than others. Why is that? Management! Handle your resources, and they will get the job done for you.

Managers who don't delegate usually get lost in the details. That is a prescription for not seeing the big picture. Effective leaders are goal oriented, focusing more on results than on methods. Too much supervision destroys individual initiative and creates a dependency that makes both the supervisor and supervisee less effective.

Training is an investment in people resources. My firm prefers to hire people just out of school. Sure, there is a tremendous training cost but, if done right (and we do it right!), a much smaller learning curve. There can never be too much effective training. Most of the successful companies I work with know this.

Set deadlines. Project deadlines are sometimes mistaken for starting dates. Break the job into multiple tasks, each with a separate deadline. Don't try to overcome human nature; learn to live with it—or work around it—and benefit from it.

CHAPTER 21

When You Are Trying to Communicate, Make Sure You Communicate

Speak, write, and illustrate in language and terms that are familiar to the people you want to adopt your ideas. Impressing at the cost of not fully transferring your ideas or knowledge will cost you the relationship at some future point in time. In the long run you will lose out, even though you might (you think) score points in the short run.

Many things that impress make communicating more difficult. Using uncommon and multisyllable terminology creates hindrances to the comprehension or instruction process. The increasingly more regular process of "justifying" both margins of letters makes letters harder to read. It certainly impresses, but is it communicating—transferring the thoughts of the writer to the reader—effectively? I think not! With modern software, many letters and memos have become slick and impersonal printed brochures or flyers. They are not read with the same personal interest a regular, typed letter used to be. We have the technology, but we have to choose when and where it is appropriate to use. And we should resist overkill.

The most effective communicators clearly articulate the obvious. They make the difficult simple. Longer is not necessarily better. The Gettysburg Address took only 2 percent of the time to say compared to the speech of the featured speaker that day. And we barely remember the main orator's name.[7]

It takes work to be able to communicate. The rewards will be that your ideas will be transferred in the effective way you want and need them to be. Mark Twain once began a letter by saying, "Please excuse the long letter, but I didn't have the time to write a short one." It does take work!

Communicating is a form of persuading someone to do what he or she never thought they would do, wanted to do, or could do. It is a method of giving someone a means of rationalization.

Communication takes many forms. Body language or a facial expression can sometimes tell much more about a person than spoken words. Watch for the small signs. Fidgeting, hands in front of mouth, not making eye contact, appearing to bluff, hesitate, or vacillate—all transmit meanings. Cheap shirts give bad and sometimes false impressions. Ties that are not tied properly or that are not knotted up to the top of the collar could

---

7   Edward Everett, United States senator, governor, secretary of state and president of Harvard University spoke his 13,600-plus word oration for two hours before Lincoln delivered his 270-word address.

give weak impressions. Unpressed trousers or scuffed shoes transmit sloppy impressions.

Poor grammar and spelling likewise give bad impressions. But they also fail to effectively communicate. The reader becomes less concerned with the ideas and overly concerned with the way in which the memo or letter was written or the ideas were spoken.

CHAPTER 22
Insist on Getting All That Was Promised to You

Make sure you get what was promised. When it comes to retail purchases you can walk away dissatisfied and not buy from that place again. The same is true with a restaurant. But what about a vital supplier? It may not be so easy to stop patronizing them. In these instances, you must insist on quality and timeliness. If you don't get it and it is not an isolated instance, you must meet with the supplier to find out what causes the problems and how you can work around it.

Many times suppliers have schedules that you can find out and use. If you always need rush printing, and it never seems to be fast enough, find out the reason. (Note: Part of the reason can be yours by always waiting until the last minute, but that is not for this chapter.) I buy a great deal of printing on paper that the printer doesn't always carry in stock. I found out that the printer can place an order for special printing paper up until 3:00 p.m. to get delivery the next day. I now make sure our orders arrive to the printer before 3:00 p.m. This is not too big an adjustment on our part and gets us delivery a day sooner. A place we buy software from always seems to be out of stock on featured items. Through some inquiries, we found out its ordering procedures stipulate the placing of orders for out-of-stock items only on Thursdays, for delivery the following Wednesday. This does not seem reasonable to me nor does it meet my needs. I now buy elsewhere, for a little higher price, and get immediate delivery—completely free of aggravation and eliminating my constant checking with the supplier to see if my order came in.

When you are supervising someone, it is absolutely essential that you get exactly what you want, the way you want it, and when you want it. Supervising, managing, and training are all synonymous when someone is doing something for the very first time. If you are willing to accept less than 100 percent of what you want, you have just lowered the standard—forever. Most people will remember how something is done the first time they do it and repeat it that way in the future. Also, any standards you are trying to set will not be honored because it will seem nothing more than the opening statement in a "bargaining" session. You must develop your own standards and not be willing to accept less. You must also develop an internal consistency and not deviate from it in matters of exigency.

It is always easier and faster to do something yourself. In matters you can delegate, the act of delegation means that, for the long haul, you found a better way to use your time. By training today, you are making a decision that your time will be better spent in the future, and it is worth the "cost" of training.

Training time represents a conscious decision to invest time today for benefits in the future. It is an investment. It is also a decision not to mortgage your future with work that can be delegated that you haven't delegated.

Don't ruin your investment by being unable, or unwilling, to spend the little bit (or great amount) of extra time now to insist on getting the job done exactly the way you want it. If you're committed to growing, working smarter and being more effective then spend the time now to get it done right.

Never relax your standards. Never! If you settle for less, even once, you will never get what you really want and need, not for ten times of insistence.

CHAPTER 23
Give Value

Always give the client what he or she pays for, or more. Never less! This applies to product as well as service, to results as well as efforts.

Project yourself as the client. Does what you give the client tell what he or she needs to know, must know, and didn't already know? Do you provide it quickly, easily, and in a timely manner? Would you use you or your firm if you were doing the hiring? Your security with the client comes from performance, not from idle or unkept promises and less than perfect work.

Undercommit and overperform.

I once hired a salesman and based his compensation on new business received plus existing business retention. His job was not just to bring in new clients but to make sure they were happy and satisfied. I told him to do for my company what he expected from everyone he patronized.

When you think of superior customer service you think of Disney World and Nordstrom and Ritz Carlton. Teach your personnel to act the same way.

CHAPTER 24
Know Where You and Your Associates Sit on the Organization Chart

Don't think you are more important than you actually are. See where you sit in relation to everyone else. Who is your mentor? Who looks up to you? Who are your peers and, perhaps, your competition? If you don't know, it won't matter too much because you will be passed by so many times that you will not only look like you are standing still but retreating.

Draw up four organization charts. On the first one, you should put down what you think the actual organization order is. On the second, put down what you think your boss (or your partners or clients) believes the organization chart is. On the third, put down how you think your subordinates view it. And on the fourth, put down what you think it should be. With all four in front of you, try to get a perspective on your job and how it fits within the organization. Now try to set up a realistic chart that could be used as an attainable goal. Concurrently, you could ask subordinates to prepare similar charts to get a better handle on your firm and on your and their duties within it.

By having subordinates prepare organization charts, you can get a good feeling of how they perceive themselves and their role, and you might uncover latent ambitions. I have found this a very valuable technique in helping clients evaluate their staff and even their children who are working in the business. It also can be a strong indication of each employee's interest in the company and what he or she is doing there.

Preparing the charts does not have to take a lot of skill. It can be drawn freehand. Don't get caught up in the graphics or software techniques. The important thing is to get the thoughts down so they could be reviewed and discussed—and show a big picture.

PART IV

Efficiency

CHAPTER 25
Understand Everything You Do

Never proceed if you don't fully understand what has to be done, why it is necessary, and what the objectives are. Many times I get a new client because the former accountant told the client to do something that the client didn't fully understand and that didn't work, but the client did it anyhow because they felt the accountant knew more than they did in that area. That's bull! It is your money, and the consequences for mistakes are yours, not anyone else's. If it doesn't make complete sense, it's probably wrong—the adviser doesn't fully know what he or she is telling you to do, they might not have all the information, or maybe wasn't quite listening to what you said. Otherwise, why is it so hard for your adviser to explain it to you so you understand it?

Put what you do in perspective. For instance, let's say someone is going to Wrigley Field in Chicago. What directions do you give him? If he is coming from Europe, first you have to give directions to the United States, then to Chicago, and then to Wrigley Field. If you gave him the Chicago directions first, he might never get to Wrigley Field. You use different maps. You start with the big picture and end up with the little, narrow picture … leave Europe first and get to the exact place last. Both are important but at different stages. The trick is to know when to use either discipline.

Running a business is one of the most difficult things someone can do. It can be made a lot easier if the manager deals with both the big-picture items and the smallest items. Leave the in-between stuff to the staff people. The big picture sets the tone, vision, culture, and direction for the organization. The smallest item is at the final sale or delivery level to the customer. Understand the company from the standpoint of the customer—how the customer is treated and what he or she sees when making a purchase. If you can't see things from the vantage point of the customer, you shouldn't be in business. Actually, that is not a small item, but possibly your most important item. Treat it so!

Know when your train has stopped. Don't chase dead causes, programs, or ideas. Don't make the last stop your last stop.

CHAPTER 26
Do What's Expected in an Unexpected Way

Simple things done in a different manner will make them seem more interesting ….. and important.

Prepare models for a company downsizing and ask for justification why it should not take place. Ditto but do it during good times when a need is not felt! It is amazing that when business really gets bad, companies can fire 10 percent to 15 percent of their personnel without any loss of production. Why did it take the bad times to cause that? Imagine how much more successful the company would have been if they had acted sooner. Note: If sales declines reduced the need for output, then the laid-off people would not be needed, but that is not usually the case with wholesale layoffs—it is usually a poor profit outlook.

Instead of giving an employee a performance review, ask him or her to justify their position and compensation level.

Make the image reality. If you can't back up what you say with what you do, you won't have who to do it for, for too much longer. Work hard at creating an impression and harder at keeping it by meeting and exceeding your commitments.

Everything counts. People judge you by what's important to them, by their agenda. You never know what shapes their thoughts. Try to anticipate their agenda and prepare for it, and your value will be increased.

You must always act with attention to every detail. You can, and should, delegate many details, but it should be done with the care and attention that you give to everything else you do. The best researched report can give a negative impression if the client's name is misspelled or there are too many typos or necessary steps are not thought out completely.

How many times have you called a customer service department and been put on hold for a dozen or so minutes? How many times have you called and reached someone immediately who understood your problem and was able to help you while you were talking to him or her? Who would you patronize again and again and recommend at every opportunity?

What do you do when you finally call a new supplier to place an order and then get put on hold for a couple of minutes? You hang up!

One of the things I do is place all reports and tax returns I review and sign off on into the mailing envelope. This gives me a moment to examine whether the client's name is spelled correctly and whether the address is the right one. Negative feelings result when a client moved, and the report is sent to the old mailing address. It also delays the report's receipt. Great embarrassment and bad feelings are created if a tax return is sent to the address of the client's ex-spouse or to current spouse that the client doesn't want to see the return just yet. Also, there is a great deal of satisfaction from placing the reports and tax returns in the envelopes because it means the job is completed!

Have you ever noticed how nicely polished your shoes are when they are picked up from the shoe repair shop? Do you make that little extra effort for your customer?

Ignore the walls. Have you ever seen an architect make rough drafts to redesign an existing office? They ignore the walls! It's amazing what you could accomplish when you remove the boundaries. Expand the walls of your ideas and dreams!

If you have to tell someone when you've done something great, maybe it ain't so great. But it also isn't so bad at the end of a meeting to state that it was a good meeting and summarize what had been accomplished, discussed, and decided.

CHAPTER 27
Identify the Most Important Thing You Have to Do, and Only Concentrate on That Until It's Done

You can only do one thing at a time, so why not spend it doing the "Most Important Thing" (MIT) you have to do. Also recognize that no one can do two things at the same time—not even you!

Identifying the MIT might not be easy to do. Most of us have multiple priorities and pressures. You can identify it as "the thing that will cause you the most anxiety if it is not done," or "the thing that will most likely cause you to wake up in the middle of the night in a cold sweat," or "the thing that you ran out of excuses for explaining why it was not done so you said it was completed, but there was some trouble getting it typed, so it will be delivered tomorrow," or "the thing that must be done before you leave for a vacation," or simply "the thing that is the most important project for your most important client, customer, boss, or lifelong goal."

Whatever the MIT is, identify it clearly to yourself and dedicate yourself to getting it done before you start your next MIT.

You can keep a project list or folder of "To Do" items. (This also appears in a later chapter.) Then go over the list and identify the top ten MITs. Never identify more than ten[8] items as your MIT. Set deadlines for those ten items, keeping in mind that you will only be taking care of one item at a time. Don't clutter your mind with too many things that you know you won't be able to do. If it must be done, you will be working on it.

There can only be one MIT.

If your project list is too long, ask yourself if it is essential that a particular project needs to get done. Six months from now, will you regret not having done this project? If the answer is no, then it is not an MIT. If the project is essential, try to figure out how you can delegate it to someone else or how you can break it into a series of smaller projects spread among a

---

8   Actually 10 is probably too many also. Too many items make the list a place where you put down open items so you could feel in control and probably won't look at the list for quite a while, until you have to add other things you didn't and won't get to. More than ten MITs makes nothing an MIT. The MIT is usually your most important and most urgent thing. How can you have more than one MIT? The "M" refers to one item, not a multiple.

number of people or how you can just do it yourself and get it done!

Organize your work into manageable chunks. Any job can be broken down into smaller pieces.

Doing it now is the best way to get the job done.

Every decision not made (that is, when the decision first comes to your attention) is a mortgage against your future. At some point in the future, you will no longer be in control of your time—that will be when that delayed item must be done, and you would rather not be working on it.

Many people don't like loans. So why mortgage your time future?

When you are at a meeting, start with the most important item, not the one that is easiest to discuss or cross off the list as completed.

Stephen R. Covey said in *First Things First* that "the main thing is to make the main thing the main thing!"

When you run your life, do you keep focused on the MIT? At year end do you review your beginning of the year resolutions and find that most did not get done? Do you wonder why you could not have found the time to do what you thought, at the beginning of the year, were the most important things you wanted to do? Stop wondering, and *do them*! Did you ever hear an elderly person tell you his regrets: the "haven't dones," the "wish I hads," and the "would haves?"[9] Do you want to be saying the same things when you are their age? Late-in-life regrets are not for what you did wrong, but are for what you did not do!

In business, you have to choose regularly what you "must do" over what you "would most like to do." Both are important. Make the "must do's" the "most like to do's," and then you'll have fewer regrets and become more effective and have more fun.

Another way to put what you do in perspective is to ask yourself what your return on investment (of time) is. Is the dividend worth the investment?

Many not-so-successful people always assume they have unlimited time to get all their work done, and so they do what they would rather do than what they need to do at that moment. Successful people focus on the MIT and get it done.

---

9   When Joe Torre declined the offered contract and resigned as manager of the Yankees, a reporter asked him what his biggest mistakes or regrets were as a manager. His response was that he did not regret the things he did that did not turn out—his regrets were the things he should have done, but didn't!

CHAPTER 28
Don't Be Late

Always start meetings on time, and be on time for others' meetings. When you come late, others will control the meeting, your calendar, and your time. You can't leave before the end if it was your shortcoming that caused a meeting to start late. On the other hand, being on time and starting promptly puts you in complete control of the agenda. And it allows you to leave when you need to go to your next meeting, or to just get out of there!

Punctuality is respect for the time of others. They notice it and respond to it.

There is nothing wrong with being five minutes early. Just be prepared to wait by having something to do while you are waiting. You should look at the free time as a bonus to do something you ordinarily wouldn't have been able to do. I carry a small scratch pad with me with a list of ideas I want to develop. If I find myself with a few extra minutes I look at it as an opportunity to develop those ideas, which are on my

"Important but Not Urgent" list[10]. Also, the difference between being five minutes early and five minutes late is ten minutes of strain on your nervous system.[11]

The job can never be okay if it's not delivered on time: Part of the job requirement is a timely completion and delivery. If a job is delivered late and can't be used or serve its purpose, it can't be satisfactory. Missing the boat will cause you to miss an opportunity that can never be made up.

Time thieves: People who come late to a meeting or make someone wait are stealing time. When someone comes late, most people stop the meeting and bring the latecomer up to date regarding the meeting. This creates a penalty for those who were on time and no penalty for the latecomer. I try not to stop a meeting to brief the latecomer. You would be surprised how few people come late to future meetings. When a price is paid for tardiness, a sharp respect will be developed for your time.

Oh, and show up! Many times the job is awarded to the person who shows up—not the smartest, best, fastest, brightest, or shiniest. I have seen the available person succeed far more times than the one who isn't there.

---

10   From *Getting Things Done*, by Edwin Bliss. One of the best time management books I ever read, and highly recommended.

11   This thought is not mine originally. I remember reading it somewhere but couldn't find the original source. My apologies to whomever it was.

CHAPTER 29
Respect Time

Time is an irretrievable asset. Once it is here, it is gone. And no matter who you are, you are no richer or poorer in the time bank than anyone else. However, there are many ways of using your withdrawals to maximum advantage.

Organize yourself to make the best use of your strengths and to minimize the disruption or waste caused by your weaknesses. For example, if you find you do your best writing, planning, or thinking work in the morning, schedule that time for your most important projects. Use your afternoons for the meetings. Arrange for some of your writing, planning, or thinking work time to be without any interruptions. Hold your calls. Don't look at your Outlook® in-box. Close your door. Go to another office, the library, or an empty conference room. Some people I know get to their office at six or six thirty in the morning to get a jump on the day. Others I know stay after hours, or come back after dinner to get some quiet time. Whatever your style or choice, carve out that quiet time when you are most likely to be your most productive. This will assure you that you can get done some of what you must get done.

Learn to use the telephone better. When you get a call, ask what you can do for the caller, not how the caller is. He or she might tell you or respond by asking you how you are, and so on. When you make a call, leave short, action-oriented messages (as long as it is not a confidential matter) with specifics of the kind of response expected.

One of the types of people I can't stand is what I call the compulsive "return-the-caller." As a CPA I am out of my office a lot, oftentimes at meetings where it is not possible to receive calls (unless they are emergencies). When I call someone who is not in, I usually leave a message telling him when and where to call me back. The compulsive "return-the-caller" typically calls me back as soon as he or she gets my message, never considering that I will not able to take the call. It then becomes my job to return the call and possibly get tied up in telephone tag when they simply could have called me when I said I would be available.

Business lunches are an effective way to kill two birds with one stone. You have to eat anyway, so why not do it with someone you need to meet with? The problem with business lunches is that they can be dragged out, especially if the person you are with has a second meeting in the area of the restaurant an hour after you would like to end the lunch. What I do is tell the person I am having lunch with what I want to talk about and what time I must end the lunch. This keeps the meeting on track and doesn't allow your lunch mate to dawdle.

Another thing I try to do is set the pace. If you ask for the menu immediately and say you want to order and get that out of the way, the food will be served much sooner than if you don't pick up the menu until you get your business out of the way. Never drink at lunch. It will dull the senses for the afternoon, and sometimes the senses don't need much help to dull. I also try not to eat anything other than fresh fruit for dessert if I am having dessert. The rich, sugar-laden cakes and pastries have the same dulling "I'd rather be doing anything other than work" effect as alcohol. And who can afford the calories?

Take the time to read instructions or directions. It always takes longer when you don't know where you are going.

Take the time to plan and prepare. Many jobs can be short-circuited when you know exactly what has to be done, the order it will be done, and how it will be done.

Learn to say *no*! Practice in front of a mirror or when you are driving. Much time can be saved by not doing that which you ought not to do.

Know what you are trying to accomplish when you do something. One of my bosses once read the entire tax handbook that we get each year at the beginning of the tax season. Years later he was still quoting outdated laws. He should have spent his time familiarizing himself with the index and then simply looked up questions as they arose.

Stop wasting other people's time, and you will stop wasting your own time. If you think you are being effective when you barge in on someone to get a quick answer for yourself, you are wrong. This takes your time away from what you were doing, breaks your momentum, and gives a license for that person to later interrupt you.

You have to organize and plan your time so that you can get everything done that you have to do. Your business should be organized so that everyone will have time to do what they need to do to make things easier for you. If you could carve out your own job, what would it be? If you really examine how you spend your time, you might see that much less is spent on doing things than on attending meetings, talking on the phone, responding to e-mails, supervising those under you, and planning what you have to do. With that in perspective, review how you spend your time to maximize your effectiveness. Give yourself the proper time to do what only you can do, and then delegate everything else.

CHAPTER 30
Always Do Your Best

No matter what you do, people measure and evaluate you. In your business or personal life, you are sized up by how you conduct yourself, and you never know how it can help or hurt you.

My sons' friends and neighbors' children are people I've seen grow up. I've watched them develop from infants to adults. I've formed opinions all along the way, and at some point these opinions count when I am asked to hire or recommend them for jobs or to counsel them on the future course of their lives. The stupid things kids do might result in an unfavorable impression I will carry with me about those kids. Also affecting my opinion will be the outstanding things they did. For example, one of them might have impressed me by asking my opinion of what books he should read, or by talking about the type of books he reads, or by the regularity with which he reads, or by the speed with which he read and returned (or did not return) books I loaned to him. The seriousness with which he approached his responsibilities also affected my opinion. Having enthusiasm about his job or, conversely, a lack of interest, also shaped my thinking. Studying hard for exams, or partying beforehand, also affected my thinking.

You never know what might develop and who you might need to help you. Doing your best in everything you do will create favorable impressions as well as the satisfaction of a job well done. Many outwardly successful people I know purposefully show disdain when they have to do a seemingly mundane task. This negatively affects my opinion of them, making me feel that if they ever did anything they didn't think was up to their standards, or level, they might not give it their all. This affects my opinion of so-called professionals such as doctors or lawyers. Perhaps my matter, which is important to me, might not be perceived as important to them.

Take pride in your work. I will always choose a person who takes pride in his or her work over someone who is more knowledgeable. I feel internal motivation and ego will overcome the perfunctory performer whenever it counts.

A professional is a professional in everything he or she does. Persistence, determination, tenacity, and perseverance are what win, not intelligence, knowledge, or genius. It's good to combine everything. The greatest waste is unsuccessful or underachieving talented people, who usually lack drive.[12]

"Neither snow, nor rain, nor heat, nor gloom of night, stays these couriers from the swift completion of their appointed

---

12 I know. this is similar to Calvin Coolidge's "Press On," used in chapter 10, but it fits in here so nicely.

rounds."[13] This quote is on the façade of the NYC General Post Office Building and should apply to everyone assuming a responsibility to get a job done.

No matter how hard you work or how late you stay or how much you are rushed to get the job done, if there is an error, it will have to be redone, and you will not be recognized for the great job you did under extraordinary conditions. Rather, you will be thought of as not "getting the job done" in a pinch, i.e., someone who can't be counted on. *Do it right the first time*, and self-check your work until you are satisfied it is without error.

---

13   Adapted from Herodotus and found in *Bartlett's Familiar Quotations*.

CHAPTER 31
If You're Having a Party, Have a Party

Concentrate on what you are doing. Work hard, but also play hard. When you are relaxing, or suppose to be relaxing, relax. Don't think about the office or business or that big order or big client.

We all need to unwind. Learn to relax and have fun. You can't be uptight all the time and then expect to perform optimally. Recharge your batteries. Do preventative maintenance on your mind and body.

Take vacations where you have a complete change of scenery. Grab days off and just hang around the house catching up on whatever needs to be, or should be, done.

When you take time off, don't call the office. If you do, your staff will save all the big problems for you, and you will never unwind. If your office knows you are away and unreachable, they will make decisions on their own. How many problems can arise that can't wait five to ten days for you to return? People know that people take vacations. The wait will be allowed. And if it can't wait, they will accept the judgment of a staff person that they ordinarily wouldn't speak to if you were around or were reachable.

I have found that if I am on vacation and for some reason call my office to check on something, my receptionist or assistant will then tell every caller from that point on that I am on vacation but might call in, and they will give me their message. Now, everyone I don't call back will be upset because they were expecting it. Never, ever, call in when you are on vacation ... unless you truly want upset clients.

CHAPTER 32
Avoid Clutter

Keeping things in order will save you time and reduce pressure, because you will always be able to easily put your hands on what you need. You will never waste time looking for something. The time it costs to maintain reasonable order will pay back great dividends. Also, people are immensely impressed with, and gain great confidence in, those who are masters of what they do, and those who have the information they need easily accessible.

Read your mail, newspapers, and magazines as you get them, not as you accumulate them, and certainly not just before you are cleaning up your office. Read and then discard! Do not save anything that can be retrieved in the normal course of events from another source, including a library, database, or the Internet.

One exception to discarding what you read ASAP after you read it is if you think you will need it for an "idea" or "future projects" file. In that case, rip it out after you've read it and put it in that file, or, better, scan and save it on your hard drive (appropriately indexed and backed up). Actually, I tried the scanning method, and it takes much more time than throwing something in a file folder. The problem is that the retrieval takes longer. But most things are never needed, and, in the long run, I save a lot more time by using file folders. But what I don't do is print something to put in the folders. What I have developed for myself is to copy and paste the digital article in a Word® file for that subject with a couple of dozen articles. So, I use both methods with a variation. That saves me the most time.

I keep a specially marked "green"[14] folder for each client on either my hard drive or on the server. Whenever I have notes from a meeting or want to save something for future reference or ideas, I file it here and discard the paper. When I prepare for a meeting with that client, I simply go through this file to develop my agenda and ideas.

The purpose of the filing is to be able to have it when you want it in the future, with the reasonable expectation of needing it in the future. Design your filing system with this in mind.

If you are like most people, you have piles of "stuff" in your office. And periodically you spend time—a part of your life—organizing those piles into other piles. That seems very important, and it can be visibly satisfying looking at the newly organized piles. However, when do you do the work represented in those piles? That is what you are being paid for, not for having the best organized and neatest piles.

---

14   In the early days of business, when we did not have digitized paperless systems and used filing cabinets, I used a green file folder that would be easily retrievable for all my notes.

A method to eliminate your hard-earned piles is to place everything, i.e., all the piles and clutter, into a box, or boxes, put the date this was done on the box, and store it somewhere out of the way. If you need something in one of the boxes, a twenty-minute journey through the box should yield that "valuable" piece of paper. You can expect that you will go through the boxes three times within the next six months. That hour will be a lot less time than what you would spend "organizing" those piles and still not have it accessible. Additionally, think of all the wear and tear on your nervous system that you will save by not having to look at those piles each time you enter your office or look up from something you are working on that is really important. You should try this right now. You have nothing to lose, since nothing is being thrown away. And it takes very little time to put it in the boxes. After that's done, make sure no new clutter is accumulated by dealing with each new piece of paper as it enters your office. If you can't change your habits, and more clutter accumulates, get more boxes.

Some people feel that if they file something away, they will lose track of it. This is only so if they lose track of the entire project, client, or customer. One way of avoiding this is to make a "to do" list. Write everything down that you have to do or that has to be followed up. This will make you feel that you are in control and that you will not lose track of anything. However, the only things you actually will do are the "Most Important Things" (MITs) on your list. (See chapter 27.) Everything else will be shifted aside, list or no list. You can, though, use the list of work to be assigned as a control sheet of what everyone is doing. The main value will probably be to make you feel in control of what you need to do and then have it get off your mind to allow you to do what you need to do, unfettered by your large list of accumulated incomplete work. That is probably where the "to do" list has its value, and that is all!

Another thing you can do is cut out subscriptions to newspapers and magazines that you are not reading. You can write to the publisher any time, cancel your subscription, and even get a refund for the remaining issues. If you need to read a particular issue, you can always buy it at a newsstand or in one of those super-duper bookstores, borrow it from an associate, read it in the library, or look on the floor in the executive restroom for it. By subscribing to fewer publications, you will get to read more of what you are receiving and will get much more out of what you are doing. What I do is go to my local public library every two or three weeks and spend about a half hour flipping through about a dozen magazines I no longer subscribe to, to see what I am missing. I also spend a few minutes looking at the new books sections to get ideas of "what's new."

Respond reasonably rapidly to "things." Usually a scribbled response is better than no response. In some cases, it is actually thought of as a better response. It is more personal; it is more efficient and cost effective, and the reader knows his note got your personal attention. I have specially printed personal notepaper on which I can jot a quick note, and I hand address the envelope so I can get it off my desk quickly. I keep my personal and firm's mailing list on my PDA and can access any address, telephone fax number, or e-mail address in seconds— in much less time than it takes to put the item in a pile "to get to later." A modern alternative is to send an e-mail. A good friend, public relations pro Robert L. Dilenschneider,[15] thinks the postally mailed note works best, and I concur.

In my business, dealing with mail (postal and e-mail) is part of my job. The mail I can't delegate is dealt with as I come to it. Otherwise, I would be creating a mortgage on my future. My time would not be my own, since I would have to deal with the accumulation of mail. I usually set aside a block of time (about an hour) every other day or so to go through my mail. I don't always have the time each day, so I don't feel guilty about not getting to it. One way of keeping track of the mail you delegate is to jot it down on a follow-up list for each person who works for you. Another way is to set a deadline when you delegate it and then enter it in your Outlook® on the due date.

Make your workplace a workplace. Many desks lose their role as a work area, and instead become a storage facility or souvenir shrine. Keep your desk clean and free of anything not needed to do your job. Organize your drawers to keep things handy and in order, for frequently used items and supplies, rather than as another storage facility. Examine your physical space. Does it permit you to do your job effectively? If not, change it *now*!

Clutter comes in all shapes and sizes. People clutter up

---

15 *Power and Influence: The rules have changed.*

their minds with many inane thoughts. These range from nickel and dime matters such as being angry at a waitress who charged you for a cup of coffee she never served, to some "really important things," such as the limo company sending a sedan when everybody knows you always ride in a stretch limo. Remove these really unimportant matters from your thoughts. You waste part of your life when you get upset over things that will have no bearing on your life a week from now, let alone a year from now! Forget it! Get on with it! Life really is too short![16]

Sometimes you just can't win. When you find yourself in a situation where no matter what you do, you just can't win, shrug your shoulders and repeat after me, "I just can't win!" Repeat the phrase a few more times until you realize just that. Sometimes you just can't win! You can't go through life without ever coming across a situation where you end up on the short end of the stick through no fault of your own. Be grateful that it is not worse. Don't clutter your mind with useless, unproductive, energy-sapping thoughts.

---

16 One way of looking at things on an "importance scale" and of placing some perspective on it is to consider what effect the matter will have on you in the very near term—ten minutes, the period after the immediate present—ten months, and the long term—ten years. A great book that covers these issues is *10-10-10: 10 Minutes, 10 Months, 10 Years—A Life Transforming Idea*, by Suzy Welch. You can also read my review of her book at Amazon.com.

CHAPTER 33
Bill Promptly; Pay Promptly

When you do work for someone, they expect to pay you. The sooner you send the bill, the sooner you'll get paid. Delaying the bill reduces the person's appreciation that you expect to, and should, be paid. That person also gets an impression that maybe you are not such a good businessperson, and, maybe, just maybe, that is reflected in the work you did for them.

Many times people do not thank those working for them the way they should. One way to say thanks (a major way), is to pay their bill promptly. It is a very tangible method of saying, "Thanks for a job well done." Why do you want to deprive them of that opportunity by not billing them in a timely fashion?

Just as you like to get paid (and thanked!) quickly, so you should do also. Use your checkbook as the way to thank someone for a job well done.

CHAPTER 34
Never Trouble Trouble Till Trouble Troubles You

Perhaps the treat that got me started on this book is the following, which came from a fortune cookie many years ago.

Never trouble trouble till trouble troubles you.[17]

What does this mean? Actually, I still carry the fortune in my wallet and whip it out whenever someone talks negatively about a proposed project or rattles off a litany of what can go wrong or acts like a pessimist when optimism should prevail.

I also try not to waste time anticipating and worrying about things that are improbable and most likely will never occur, or things that can be routinely dealt with when they do come up.

---

17   Some unknown person first said this. One of the attributions I found was from John Adams.

PART V
Business Development

CHAPTER 35
Network

Keep track of each and every person you meet. And make sure each person keeps track of you! It is quite simple. All you have to do is send a Christmas or New Year's card and drop a note one other time during the year. Find out when their birthday is and send them a card or e-mail, or make a quick phone call. Send them a newspaper or magazine article that might relate to a particular person, or what he or she does, or someone you both know. If your firm has a mailing list, make sure they are on it and receive the mailings, with an occasional personal note accompanying it.

President Clinton kept track of almost everyone he met in school and then when he started working. When he decided to run for president, he had a very large group of committed friends to draw upon for support.

Meeting people can be as easy or as hard as you want to make it. You can enjoy joining organizations and meeting people, or you can dread it and instead take courses, or you can get involved in a charity as a worker instead of as a planner. As you meet people, keep track of who they are, what they do, and their interests, and keep in mind how you can help them, and they you.

Linkedin®, Facebook®, Twitter®, MySpace®, IM and other methods are making it super easy to keep track of people, but make sure you add the human element by keeping in touch other ways—not just with e-mails from time to time.

Sometimes you can help someone, and he or she could resent it, but the person would enjoy helping you. Find an opportunity where they could do you a favor. As long as it's not too time-consuming or it doesn't cost the person a favor with someone else, he or she usually would be very pleased to assist or lend a hand. You will have just created a relationship that will last. If you are called upon to do a favor for someone, try to do it where it doesn't look like it is too big of a deal for you. You don't want to create resentment. People are funny!

A good way to network is to write a column for an organization newsletter about what members are doing. I did this when I was in college, in the army, in a fraternal organization, and then in my synagogue. It's an easy way to get to meet and talk to people.

Networking means not only staying in touch with people you know, but not burning bridges or parting company on an unfavorable note. You never know who knows who, or when a distasteful event will come back to haunt you. A way to eliminate future problems is to avoid taking on something that you can't reasonably get done when it is supposed to be done.

It is possible to ask for one favor from anybody with whom you once had a positive relationship. The favor may not be granted, but the door is open for you to ask. And, surprise of surprise, you might get it. People generally like to help others. Keeping that in mind, you should save the request of a favor for something really important or meaningful. It also helps if you keep in touch.

CHAPTER 36
Establish Your Brand

You have a brand, whether you know it, want it, or believe it.

Your brand is the way you dress, respond and follow-up, your firm's evident culture, and everything about you. Your image is established by your letterhead and type style of your letters and reports, by the memos you write, by the way you speak, and by your Web site, newsletters, press releases, and publicity. How your telephone is answered and everything you do that creates a contact with anyone is a "brand moment." What is your image?

The power of a brand can be shown by who you think of when someone mentions tissues, adhesive tape, bandages, or headache relief. Or, what you think when someone says Arthur Andersen, Katrina, the Edsel, or Bear Stearns?

What do your customers or clients think of when someone says your company's name? What do you think of when you think of your firm? Do you think it is the same thing?

Communicating your brand is done whether or not you want it done.

First impressions can establish and firmly imprint your brand—your look, briefcase, unshined shoes, ragged sneakers, a pin or earrings, or your tie. Even how your business card looks affects your brand. I was given a card recently from a partner of another CPA firm, and it had dirty, worn edges. I was sorry he gave it to me instead of to a potential client that we were both trying to get.

Branding is more than a logo. It is a mind-set, a culture, a conditioning, a feeling, an image, positioning, a commitment, consistency, reliability, a level of quality, the conveyance of a feeling of security, and much more.

Branding is done by a continual, repetitive replication of the qualities your brand is built on. Hopefully some of those qualities are unique for your firm and are identified as such by your universe of clients, contacts, and acquaintances.

The value of a brand could be measured by the difference of the price/earnings ratio of Coca Cola versus a generic soda manufacturer.

How you handle your brand determines its value. You should must know what your brand is, and you must work to enhance its value.

CHAPTER 37
The Customer Is Always Right

You will never win an argument with a customer if you lose that customer, his or her goodwill, or subsequent referrals. Scoring points against an upset customer is the method to losing the game.

Part of customer service is the belief that the customer is always right. Blame the customer for something, and he or she is lost forever. Letting the customer win the point, or acknowledging that the customer is right, can keep them forever.

There is a long-established furniture store in the neighborhood where I live. You can always hear their friendly and frequent commercials on the radio. One time I asked my wife why she never goes in there. She said that she did when our oldest child was about three years old. He was yelled at for sitting on a couch. So she left and never returned. Note: This is an example of where the "brand" wasn't communicated to the people who were on the front line dealing with customers. (See previous chapter.)

Do you rate your customers? Many people concentrate only on the largest ones while either ignoring the smallest, or certainly not paying much attention to them. Good customers are not just the biggest. There might be many small customers who have recommended a lot of business to you, making their family tree of your customers quite large. A slight to one will certainly be told to the others. Also, the profit ratio might be higher for a small customer than for a large one. Sure, you have much more to lose if you lose a larger customer, in terms of volume and possible prestige, but how much from the bottom line will you lose? If you abandon a group of smaller customers, how much will you lose? Compare the two; it may not be much different.

Exception: When customer wants you to compromise your standards, morals, or honesty. Hasta La Vista! Run from them and don't look back! In this situation, the customer is always *wrong*!

CHAPTER 38
Find Your Unique Selling Proposition

In 1961, Rosser Reeves wrote and published a fantastic book, *Reality In Advertising*. It was expanded from his privately printed memoir by Ted Bates & Company, his firm. This book created the expression Unique Selling Proposition (USP).

The USP has since been cited many dozens of times by as many authors and leadership gurus, but it first grew from Rosser Reeves's method, which catapulted his advertising agency into the big leagues.

Successful businesses need something that differentiates them—it could be a product, their high quality, their delivery system, super treatment of customers, or a myriad of other qualities. And then they need to let the world know about it—they need to publicize it, advertise it, and exploit it in the marketplace to gain an advantage over their competitors.

In my experiences, I have found that many businesspeople don't clearly identify their USP—they don't have that capacity—while others trumpet it every moment of every day in everything they do. The truly successful are the ones that understand what their USP is (or USPs are), and they are able to communicate and capitalize on it.

PART VI
Negotiating

CHAPTER 39

Never Seek Total Victory …
Unless You Are in a Dark Alley
or a Courtroom

When negotiating, always let the other side walk away with something. If they get nothing out of you, he or she will build a resentment that will cost you much more at a later time, and more than likely you won't know about it.

Treat adversaries with the same dignity and respect you crave for yourself.

Negotiation is the art of getting what you want. It requires the skills of presenting data in a manner where the only conclusion could be yours.

Nothing speaks with greater assurance than a proper presentation of facts. The clearer you understand something, the easier the presentation, the easier the solution, and the easier it will be for someone else to understand what you mean or are trying to accomplish.

Draw first. Only in the cowboy movies does the good guy let the bad guy draw first. That is make-believe. You will "kill" more people if you draw first, and be "killed" less often. It is important to set the agenda. Then everything works off of your position. Being prepared is a big part. You also have to let the other side see the fruits of your preparation. As an accountant, it is easy for me to set the agenda. People expect accountants to have facts and data (usually in the form of numbers) with them. It is easy to have a projection, analysis, or even a listing of points to cover, to use as a guide or focus of the meeting. That becomes the opening round, which you have just won.

Do the work—push the pencil. One time a client of mine was offered a job to set up a United States operation for a major foreign manufacturer. The manufacturer had applied for a license to distribute a particular product line in the United States. Further inquiry turned up the fact that the license's issuance was contingent on my client heading the company, since he had the reputation and expertise to ensure the greatest chance of success. I asked my client to arrange for one final meeting, with me attending to iron out the details and the tax characteristics for the offshore owner. My client and I worked around the clock to draw up five-year projections of the new company, its product line, marketing plan, cash flow, and initial investment commitment in order for the new venture to have the greatest probability of success. The projections also established the parameters of the value my client would bring to the venture. The numbers turned out so good (and with the knowledge that it wouldn't get off the ground without my client) that we asked for, and got, a contingent arrangement that netted my client almost four times what he had previously been offered! Today, over two dozen years later, it is one of the major companies in its field and would immediately be recognizable if I mentioned its name.

Another time I was engaged to help close up a company that the Internal Revenue Service was in the process of seizing. For all intents and purposes, the company was dead. The owners were resigned to losing the business and their residences and to filing personal bankruptcy. What they particularly wanted from me was trying to work out a deal with the IRS whereby the unpaid trust fund withholding tax obligation was extinguished, so they could at least walk away from everything free of debt. In order to get a handle on the situation, the assets, cash flow, and value of an orderly liquidation over a forced closure, I had the client give me a crash course about their business. I prepared what I felt was a realistic projection, which then became a plan to save the company. When I met with the IRS revenue officers, I showed it to them and asked for a small amount of time to see if we could pull off any of it. The plan was as elaborate as any that I had ever done, and (maybe in deference to the work I did!) they allowed a short period of time. Well, we (that is, the client) did it. It is ten years later and the company is thriving. By the way, it took over five months after my meeting with the IRS agents until the first dollar was paid toward the arrearages! But the IRS was eventually paid in full with interest.

Find the hidden agenda. Another part of negotiating is to get the other side to articulate their thoughts and hidden (sometimes even to themselves) desires to you. Their prejudices. Their fantasies. Their agenda. Their real agenda. It is not easy, but if you can find out what the other side *really* wants, you can structure the deal. Again, as a CPA regularly dealing in these matters, I developed a knack of finding these things out. People seem to be relaxed when they talk to a CPA, not like when they speak to an attorney, when they are on guard every minute of the time. What can a CPA do to hurt? And they might even offer an idea or two to save a buck in taxes. It is possible to come up with a deal that satisfies both parties. You just need to know what each one wants, and it is usually not what each one might believe.

I once had to negotiate the purchase of a business for a client. The amount needed was quite a few million dollars. When I met with the seller, it turned out that he did not want to sell but felt that he couldn't continue in business in his undercapitalized state. He really needed cash to set up a sales force to expand into new markets. As it turned out, my client was in a related industry and had a sales organization with offices across the United States. We ended up negotiating an exclusive sales agency for my client. No funds were used to buy the equipment-intensive business. The person who started the company kept his baby, and my client kept his cash. Both sides' needs were met, more happily than if the originally stated plan was followed.

Always make sure you understand your opponent's position. The more you ask, the more you will be able to understand his or her views. Also, by letting an opponent have his say, he feels you are more fully considering his needs.

The easiest time to negotiate is when you are completely bluffing. In that situation, you cannot back down or give in. It is an "all or nothing" situation. A resolve not to give in or compromise is usually taken as strength and can cause slight cracks in your opponent's armor that you can exploit to a win.

The hardest time to negotiate is when you must do the deal and have no other choices, and you just don't want to screw up the deal.

The fun time is where there are two equals in battle (the hypothetical willing buyer and willing seller), and both are equally inclined to negotiate or not negotiate. But how many times has that really happened?

You should always know your fallback position. Always consider what will happen if the deal does not get done. Where will you stand? This should be mapped out, so you will know the next step you will take if the current deal doesn't get done. Sometimes, in considering the fallback position, you come up with alternatives that might lead you on a different, and better, road.

It is also important to leave yourself a way out if the negotiation doesn't go the way you want. It also helps if you have left your opponent a way back in. In this manner, you have kept the door open for future dealings.

Be a gracious loser … and an even more gracious winner. Why not?

A quick word about lawsuits. They are war. And there you must do whatever you need to do to win—and take no prisoners. Also, in a courtroom, the better person or cause does not always win—the better lawyer always wins. And the better lawyer is also usually the best prepared.

CHAPTER 40
Don't Ask a Question When You Know the Answer Will Embarrass Someone

The best way to make an enemy is to lead him into embarrassing himself. Others who are present will also be placed in an embarrassing position. How do you win when that happens?

Don't pounce and don't gloat. You will draw even more sympathy for your target and further embarrassment for the other attendees, lessening any advantage you may have had by the superior knowledge.

If it is an adversarial situation, why is it so important to force the issue? Wouldn't it be more advantageous to you if your opponent has a misconception? If it is a friendly situation, you have been given an opportunity to teach and instruct. Do it tactfully.

People shown up tend to try to get even—at some point—and it is usually at their choosing and advantage.

In his autobiography, Benjamin Franklin tells how he broke himself of his argumentative propensity. He adopted a reverential mannerism and suggested that, even though the other person seemed to know the subject quite well, perhaps there was another way of handling the situation. He then got converts to his viewpoints, without his discussion mate knowing Franklin got his way.

CHAPTER 41
Cut Your Losses

The first loss is always the cheapest.

When you realize you are in a bad situation, get out of it as quickly as possible. Whatever the cost, it will be the least expensive, in cash and in time, and will give you your future opportunity energy back.

If you have to do something unpleasant, putting it off just prolongs the agony.

Many times the first settlement offer in a litigation is the best offer. You might eventually get more if you don't lose, but what about the loss due to the wear and tear on your nervous system and energy level, as well as loss of the use of the money, and the continued out-of-pocket cost to prolong the action?

Sometimes something is prolonged out of spite or personal animosity. That is not what business should be about.

Many times not cutting losses is the result of unrealistic expectations, not knowing or having all the facts, not understanding the other side's position, and not recognizing the big picture.

PART VII
You

CHAPTER 42
Be Proud of a Worn Dictionary

A worn dictionary, Bible, favorite book of poems, or other reference source means it has been used frequently.

Use all the tools you can get your hands on, and use them often. You certainly can't know everything, but you can, and should, know how to find out the things you don't know and need to know. Every once in a while, peruse the reference sections of your local library and bookstores. You'll be surprised at the wealth of information at your fingertips.

CHAPTER 43
Don't Smoke

Practice good health policies. Don't smoke. Don't drink excessively. Don't drink and drive. Don't drive and text or answer e-mail. Watch your diet and waistline. Exercise regularly. Wear your seat belt. Check your smoke detectors. Vacation regularly. Get a proper amount of sleep. Nap if you can. Don't ride when you can walk. If you are hungry between meals, eat an apple or other piece of fruit; not a candy bar. Take a walk or do some exercises instead of taking a coffee break.

Make time for yourself to relax—unwind, goof off, let off some steam. Stress builds up unless we find ways to put it in its place. Small moments can rid you of large amounts of unproductive energy. Every once in a while reward yourself with something special that you would not ordinarily have bought. You can even make that the goal for doing something special or something that you detested doing but finally tackled. Read for pleasure and escapism. See a stupid movie that you know you would enjoy. Watch *The Sound of Music*, *The Godfather*, *Pretty*

Woman, It's a Wonderful Life, or whatever other movie you've always enjoyed, one more time.

I have found that the best way to deal with an unpleasant job is to get it done as quickly as possible. It never ends up as bad as I thought it would be, and I use up much more energy worrying about it than dealing head-on with it. You can also break up an unpleasant job into many small functions, which make doing it much easier, and think about all the satisfaction you'll get each time one of the smaller pieces is completed Note: breaking up a large job into smaller tasks seems to be a recurring theme for me—it is, and it works—and I have been very successful with it.

Get some fresh air. Breathe deeply.

Stretch!

Watch the fat.

Learn your sleep patterns. Try to sleep in accordance with your natural REM sleep cycles. These can be measured, and then you can take advantage of the information you've garnered. Tell yourself when you get into bed that you will wake up two minutes before your alarm is set to go off. And you will!

Get routine medical exams. This includes your skin, eyes, and teeth. What is routine for one person may not be for another. Settle in on what is routine for you, and schedule it as you would any other important meeting. The president of the United States does.

Be aware of what your body says to you. Usually it says that if you don't take a break every once in a while, it will take it for you (but under less pleasant circumstances).

If you don't do it voluntarily, you will end up doing it involuntarily—when you recover from a heart attack or are being treated for lung cancer or diabetes.

Appreciate your good health, and don't take it for granted.

CHAPTER 44
Have a Teddy Bear or Cat

Don't take yourself too seriously.

Talk to your teddy bear or cat or dog or whatever. (Author's note: most stores have special sections selling "whatevers.") It is pretty hard to get lost in your own importance when you say things out loud to a teddy bear. It also lets you hear how your thoughts sound. It is a good way to rehearse developing thoughts and ideas.

CHAPTER 45
Order the Soup du Jour

Why does the soup du jour always taste different? Even when you order it from the same place two or three days in a row, it always tastes different.

Life is full of surprises. Don't expect things to not change. Try new things. Life can be much more interesting if there are constantly new things for you to taste and try.

Improvement and innovation both mean change, and can only come if there is change in what is presently being done. Leaders and managers who say they want change have to be willing to pay for it. The cost is for training, retooling, measurement, buy-in, and the *support* of the project.

When instituting a new procedure or project or change, there will be dysfunction, lack of enthusiasm, possible high error rates, mixed communication, conflicts in company culture, and half-assed attempts at accountability. This has to be considered beforehand when deciding on the program and can be offset by a strong leadership commitment, evidenced by strong communication of the need for buy-in by *everyone* on the management team.

The broader your interests, the greater your opportunity for enjoying new things—and yourself.

CHAPTER 46
Call Your Aunt

You should take some time to smell the flowers.

Calling your aunt every once in a while cannot be much of a burden on you, but look at all the joy it will bring.

Every once in a while call an old friend, or an old friend's widow(er). It brings joy to at least two people—them and you.

Volunteer—to help someone personally, or in an organization that helps people. Visit or call ill neighbors, or church, mosque, or synagogue members.

Buy a present or send a card or flowers for no reason at all. They even have preprinted cards like that. Buy crazy gifts for people you know. I once got my sister-in-law a left-handed ruler, and I always have packages of baseball cards and easy-to-learn magic tricks in my office to hand out to children that are dragged there by their parents when they can't find a sitter when they come to meet with me.

It costs very little to create tremendous joy when you really care.

Everyone has a history. No one was born fully grown like Venus. Try to understand where each person came from, and what he or she has been through. Asking elderly relatives about their youth (assuming they are not the type of people who tell anyone in sight about it over and over and over) can be very enlightening for you, and you'll be doing a good deed besides.

CHAPTER 47
Fear and Love God

Following God's teachings can be as easy as applying the Golden Rule to your business dealings:

Thou shall love your neighbor as yourself.
Leviticus 19:18

What you do not want done to yourself, do not do to others.
Confucius

What is hateful to you, do not do to your fellow.
Hillel (70 BCE to 10 CE)

All things whatsoever you would that men should do to you, do you to them.
Matthew 7:12

None of you truly believes until he wishes for his brother what he wishes for himself.

> Number 13 of Imam
> "Al-Nawawi's Forty Hadiths"

Do unto others as you would have others do unto you

> The way I learned it when I was a kid.

The Ten Commandments isn't so bad either. So too for the rest of the Bible.

Regular attendance at your church, synagogue, mosque, or meeting house also is not so bad, and can be pretty good!

CHAPTER 48
Spend Quality Family Time

Your family is the most precious possession you have. Treat it so! When you are with your spouse or children, focus in on them. Don't let your mind wander about business.

No one dies wishing they spent more time with their business!

ABOUT THE AUTHOR

Edward Mendlowitz is a certified public accountant and a partner with WithumSmith+Brown in New Brunswick, NJ. He is the author of sixteen professional books and the editor of four others. Mr. Mendlowitz has written hundreds of business and financial articles and has been quoted in almost every major newspaper in the United States, and he is on the panel of experts for *Bottom Line/Personal* newsletter. He has taught in the MBA program at Fairleigh Dickinson University and is admitted to practice before the United States Tax Court. The American Institute of Certified Public Accountants has accredited him in business valuation, has certified him in financial forensics and as a personal financial specialist, and has presented him with the Lawler Award for the best article in the 2001 *Journal of Accountancy*.

BOOKS BY
EDWARD MENDLOWITZ

Successful Tax Planning (4 editions)

Tax Loopholes

The Biggest Mistakes Taxpayers Make and How to Avoid Them

J.K. Lasser's How to Profit from the New Tax Laws

Special Report: New Tax Traps/New Opportunities

Aggressive Tax Strategies

New Business Kit, How to Start and Operate a Business in New Jersey (six editions), coedited with Peter A. Weitsen and Frank R. Boutillette

Mendlowitz Weitsen LLP Resource Manual, Classic Edition coauthored with Peter A. Weitsen and Frank R. Boutillette

Mendlowitz Weitsen LLP Resource Manual, Volume 2 coauthored with Peter A. Weitsen and Frank R. Boutillette

Running a More Exciting and Profitable Accounting Business, coauthored with Peter A. Weitsen and Frank R. Boutillette

Introducing Tax Clients to Additional Services

How to Run a More Exciting and Profitable Accounting Business Seminar handbook, coauthored with Frank R. Boutillette

Estate Planning 2005 Edition, coauthored with Peter A. Weitsen

Financial Planning Guidebook, 2005 Edition

Managing Your Tax Season

The Adviser's Guide to Family Succession Planning

Contributor to the 1981, 2005, and 2009 editions of *The Corporate Controller's Manual* (Pub. by Warren, Gorham & Lamont, and Thomson Reuters).

Contributor to *Representing Professional Athletes and Teams* (1980 Practicing Law Institute).

Contributing editor to PPC's *1998/1999 706/709 Deskbook (Estate and Gift Taxes)*

Contributing editor to the *2005 and 2009 AICPA Management of Accounting Practice Handbook*.

Other books

One Minute Dvar Torah Years 1–4

PROGRAMS BY EDWARD MENDLOWITZ

Ed Mendlowitz is available to consult with clients, present all-day educational programs, and as a keynote speaker on a variety of subjects, including business succession planning and family wealth transfers, valuing a business, business management and stress testing, and leadership skill development.

Programs are listed on my website: www.edwardmendlowitz.com

Mr. Mendlowitz can be reached at WithumSmith+Brown, One Spring Street, New Brunswick, NJ 08901; tel: 732 964-9329; e-mail: ed@edwardmendlowitz.com

BOOK LIST

These books are recommended reading for further ideas and discussion.

1. *The Dilbert Principle: A Cubicle's-Eye View of Bosses, Meetings, Management Fads and Other Workplace Afflictions*, by Scott Adams

2. *Corporate Lifecycles: How and Why Corporations Grow and Die and What to do About It*, by Ichak Adizes

3. *You Are the Message*, by Roger Ailes and Jon Kraushar

4. *How I Raised Myself from Failure to Success in Selling*, by Frank Bettger

5. *Who Killed Change?* by Ken Blanchard, John Britt, Judd Hoekstra, and Pat Zigarmi

6. *The One Minute Manager* by Kenneth H. Blanchard and Spencer Johnson

7. *Getting Things Done—The ABCs of Time Management*, by Edwin C. Bliss

8. *Creating Magic*, by Lee Cockerell

9. *Good to Great*, by Jim Collins

10. *Bill What You're Worth*, by David W. Cottle

11. *First Things First*, by Stephen R. Covey, A. Roger Merrill, and Rebecca R. Merrill

12. *Power and Influence—The Rules Have Changed*, by Robert L. Dilenschneider

13. *The Essential Drucker: The Best of Sixty Years of Peter Druker's Essential Writings on Management*, by Peter F. Drucker

14. *One Great Insight is Worth a Thousand Good Ideas: An Advertising Hall-of-Famer Reveals the Most Powerful Secret in Business*, by Phil Dusenberry

15. *I-Power*, by Martin Edelston and Marion Buhagiar

16. *Creative Destruction: Why Companies That Are Built to Last Underperform the Market—and How to Successfully Transform Them*, by Richard Foster and Sarah Kaplan

17. *Autobiography of Benjamin Franklin*, still in print 220 years after he died

18. *Turn Small Talk into Big Deals, by* Don Gabor

19. *The E Myth Revisited: Why Most Small Businesses Don't Work and What to Do About It*, by Michael E. Gerber

20. *Who Says Elephants Can't Dance*, by Louis V. Gerstner Jr.

21. *Jeffrey Gitomer's Sales Bible: the Ultimate Sales Resource Including the 10.5 Commandments of Sales Success*, by Jeffrey Gitomer

22. *Small is the New Big*, by Seth Godin

23. *The Goal*, by Eliyahu M. Goldratt

Marketing to Reach Buyers Directly, Second Edition, by David Meerman Scott

37. *Value Migration: How to Think Several Moves Ahead of the Competition*, by Adrian J. Slywotzky

38. *How to Attain Financial Security and Self-Confidence*, by Marvin Small. This book was published in 1953 and is long out of print but occasionally copies are available from used book dealers. I read it when I was a very young man and it provided great inspiration and was an idea factory for me and want to acknowledge the influence it had on me by listing it here and strongly recommending it along with the other books on this list. Many of the books in this list are no longer in print, but they are all available from used book dealers. Also, many of the authors in this list have more current books, but I have shown the first one I read or liked the most, or most appropriate for readers of *Power Bites*.

39. *Your Marketing Sucks*, by Mark Stevens

40. *Sam Walton: Made in America*, by Sam Walton with John Huey

41. *Jack: Straight From the Gut*, by Jack Welch with John A. Byrne

42. *The End of Marketing As We Know It*, by Sergio Zyman

There are many others and also many other books by the authors listed above. These are some of the best that come to mind. Additional books are referenced in footnotes.

You can also read some of my book reviews at Amazon.com.

Manufactured By: RR Donnelley
Breinigsville, PA USA
August, 2010